What are others saying about this book?

I0041037

Impact: Ten ways to level up your leadership

IMPACT

10 WAYS TO LEVEL UP YOUR LEADERSHIP

REBECCA HOUGHTON

Published by Rebecca Houghton

First published in 2020 in Melbourne, Australia

Copyright © Rebecca Houghton

www.boldhr.com.au

PO Box 339, Yarraville, Victoria 3013, Australia

The moral rights of the author have been asserted.

Edited by Jenny Magee

Typeset by BookPOD

ISBN: 978-0-6450511-0-0 (pbk)

ISBN: 978-0-6450511-1-7 (ebook)

A catalogue record for this book is available from the National Library of Australia

Dedication

To the members of my Level Up Your Leadership program, past, present and future — you inspire, humble, and motivate me every day. Thank you for trusting me to play a part in your success.

To my incredible, crazy-beautiful family, without whom, I'd never have had the courage.

Contents

PART ONE: Setting the Scene

PART TWO: So What, Now What?

Preface

I remember, with stark clarity, when I realised how to level up my leadership – how to be more consistently confident, strategic and have a greater impact. I was working at one of the world's largest international health funds, and my boss had just told me I didn't have a strategic bone in my body.

Geez, that hurt – and I won't deny that it still does! But what hurt more was the fact that she couldn't teach me what to do about it. I had to go away and work it out for myself, which I did – a journey that took far too long.

Ironically, a few years later, I won a coveted award for Strategy so I really should thank her. But being strategic for me was much more than having an award-winning strategy. It was about being strategic every single day so that I could have more impact; so that I could operate like a C-Suite leader.

I looked for help, but what I found was too generic. Leadership development for an experienced-but-not-executive leader simply didn't meet the mark.

I was in a weird 'no man's land' – an experienced people leader with proven operational know-how, who was too senior for 'new manager' training, but not high enough up the ladder for executive or C-Suite investment. There was definitely no MBA budget coming my way! A classic middle manager – or as I now prefer to call it – a B-Suite leader. And like many organisations, investment in B-Suite leadership development at my employer was hard to find. The assumption was that what got me here would get me there.

Like many B-Suiters, I was in the middle of a fast-paced, complex and ever-changing landscape – which of course is ten times worse today. I was senior enough for loads of responsibility but too junior for loads of information, so I filled in the gaps with assumptions and pretended confidence when, in fact, I was terrified of making a mistake.

So how did I scramble out of that B-Suite nightmare of chaos, pressure and under-confidence and into a C-Suite state of mind? I didn't become a C-Suiter – but I had the impact of one, and that's what I want to share with you.

My hard-won learnings on this pathway to impact are now yours – and they form the basis of the Level Up program that I designed for all B-Suiters who seek more impact but lack the confidence, influence or headspace to get it right. This program works, with impressive career results and even more impressive C-Suite feedback – to learn more go to www.BoldHR.com.au/level-up-your-leadership

If you are in the B-Suite today, feeling overwhelmed, uncertain or out of control, then this book is for you. I know you are carrying a hefty load and don't have the time or desire to read a massive academic tome. So this small, practical book contains ten tools that will make the greatest difference to leaders, like you, who seek to control the pace of work, create some space to think, and influence outcomes.

This book is in two sections. In Part One, we'll set the scene about B-Suite leadership. You'll get a clear handle on what impact means at this level and why it matters. You'll also identify your situation and understand what holds you back.

If you're short on time and want to cut to the chase, then the questionnaire at the end of Part One will help you to identify which actions are most appropriate to you right now.

In Part Two, you'll find those promised, practical ideas. Put them into action, and then keep coming back to the book as you progress through the key stages of B-Suite leadership.

PART ONE
SETTING THE SCENE

*Not all leaders want to become a
C-Suite executive, but they should all
be enabled to operate like one.*

All leaders are too busy – and they are getting busier.

All leaders yearn for more space to think but rarely get it.

All leaders wish it were easier to get sh*t done, but instead, it's getting more difficult.

And all leaders know they need to influence more, but rarely have the time.

All leaders want to manage the pace so they and their teams can be more productive. Their employers want this too – and employers need more of their leaders to perform like an exec, be more promotable and close the leadership gap.

> All leaders want to manage the pace so they and their teams can be more productive.

Seventy-seven per cent of organisations report a leadership gap, which is growing fast as the traditional leadership cohort of Baby Boomers retires at a rate of more than 10,000 per day (Thornton, 2018).

Are the Millennials leaping into the gap? Yes, they are, but 63 per cent of them are concerned about a lack of leadership training. Estimates are that by 2025, Millennials will make up 75 per cent of the workforce – effectively replacing Baby Boomers as the largest generation of its era. But this current and future leadership cohort don't feel fully prepared for the complexity, pace and changeable nature of leadership today.

2

Eighty-three per cent of organisations say it's important to invest in leadership development at all levels, yet only five per cent of them are doing it (Thornton, 2018).

Leadership in the era of the Baby Boomer is profoundly different from leadership today.

The complexity of our working world has sharply increased in the last decade, and so has the pace. Running so fast, we worry we have forgotten something or that we haven't thought things through well enough. We're making decisions without all the facts, all the time. Incomplete information is now the norm, so we piece the answers together and hope we are judging it right. We're juggling multiple, competing, and changeable priorities, while recognising that, no matter what we do, all plans are subject to change.

To make this work in a complex landscape, we are working across silos. Doing so achieves great things, but it also takes more time and resources – both of which are in increasingly short supply as we accelerate our drive to do more with less.

While leaders at all levels are struggling, there's a lingering sense of 'when things return to normal' that suggests a yearning for a simpler, slower and less disrupted way of life. This is the legacy of leadership in the era of the Baby Boomer – and it's one we need to shake off.

A 2019 survey by Gartner revealed that only half of all business leaders feel confident leading their teams today (Baker, 2019).

There are new rules; they're just not well-known yet.

All leaders, at all levels, need to learn to operate differently, and that requires an understanding of fundamental changes to the rules. Leadership is a game. It's not necessarily one we need to win, but we have to play to have more impact and to level up our leadership.

It's time to invest in our leaders

And that's why we need to invest in our leaders. Not in skills training, because those are out of date almost as soon as you've learned them. And not in accruing more knowledge, because Google has cornered the market there. Instead, we need to invest in the way leaders play the leadership game, well beyond merely managing teams and work.

We want them to manage teams, manage up and manage outcomes.

To make decisions in darkness and lead with confidence in chaos.

Work in the business as well as on the business.

My son is a gamer. When studying for his first significant school exam, he spent hours revising the content. And he spent an equal number of hours working out strategies to manage the exam; how to hedge his bets if he didn't know the answers, how to pace himself against the clock and how to manage his stress reaction. He worked out that about 70 per cent of his success would be down to knowing the content. The rest would be down to how he played the game. I can't fault his logic – the kid is now annoyingly good at exams.

The forces that are shaping and reshaping our corporate landscape – technology, competition, geopolitics and demographics – are continuously changing, and are more volatile and disruptive than ever. It means organisational priorities are shifting more rapidly than ever before, and leaders must accommodate those constant changes.

Leadership training will need to adjust too. Some fundamentals will still apply, but we need new leadership to meet the needs of a new normal.

Leading from the middle

When I started writing this book, I struggled with the phrase 'middle management'. The connotations are so unflattering – guardians of policy and bureaucracy who are generally complained about by front-line staff and blamed by top-line leaders.

Organisations and social scientists have long seen middle managers as a target for assigning blame, or they have hardly seen them at all. As far as many are concerned, middle managers are invisible; they barely exist (Osterman, 2009).

C-level leaders like Steve Jobs and Elon Musk have often been cited as wishing to remove middle management from the end product entirely. Big Four-led restructures are sardonically simplified into drawing a red line

> C-level leaders like Steve Jobs and Elon Musk have often been cited as wishing to remove middle management from the end product entirely.

through middle management ranks. And popular culture like 'The Office' and 'Dilbert' cartoons don't help either. Middle managers sure do get a hard time of it.

In an article in the Strategic Management Journal, Ethan Mollick wrote that the impact of variation among middle managers on firm performance is much larger than that of those individuals who are assigned innovative roles. The results also show that middle managers are necessary to facilitate firm performance in creative, innovative, and knowledge-intensive industries (Mollick, 2012).

And, quite frankly, this is no surprise because B-Suite leaders have the hardest job of all. They are responsible for managing most of the busy workload of the organisation, for day-to-day corporate performance (without which there is no year-on-year performance), for executing the strategy and for implementing change.

Middle management is like being middle class, middle-aged or a middle child. It's tough!

The evidence is overwhelming that the disparaging 'middle manager' label is a completely – and dangerously – wrong attitude for companies to have. Middle managers are one of our most valuable assets if we enable them to operate in the right mode.

Welcome to the B-Suite

What kind of B-Suite leader are you?

You're already an experienced people leader. As you own a function, a team or a cluster of teams, you are definitely not 'in the trenches', but you're not quite 'inner circle' either.

You typically don't have a say in policy development or strategic direction. Yet, it's your job to enforce those decisions, even if you – or your teams – disagree, or even object to them.

Others look up to you as a senior leader, yet you feel you are too junior to wield any real authority.

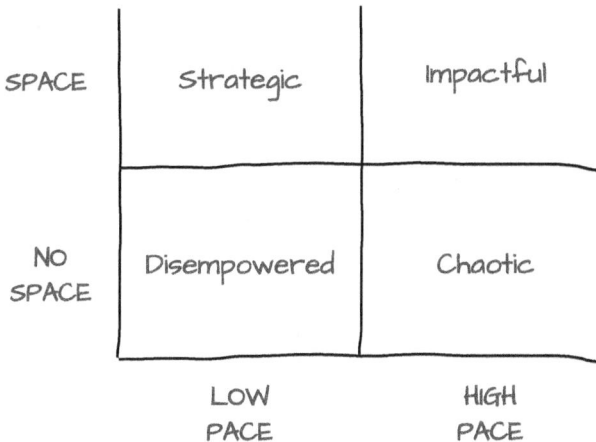

	LOW PACE	HIGH PACE
SPACE	Strategic	Impactful
NO SPACE	Disempowered	Chaotic

Figure 1: Control the pace and use the space

This model describes four situations in which B-Suite leaders often find themselves.

With high-pace, you are working so fast and furiously that your feet barely touch the ground, and low space means no time to think. In this environment, we tell others – with an expression somewhere between pride and regret – that we are soooo crazy busy. But inside, we're frequently feeling out of control and trying not to show it. Welcome to *chaos*.

Yet when the pace drops off – through a downturn, pre-merger or restructure – it's surprisingly even harder to operate. The lack of busyness undermines your sense of progress and allows you to ponder the relative lack of autonomy you have, despite the immense pressure you bear. This space is often driven by a lack of information or a lack of activity, and landing here, you can feel very vulnerable and *disempowered*.

Roles with low pace and lots of space are rare and could either reflect the nature of your work, or a moment in time when the pace eases off, and you have room to think ahead. This is when you get to be *strategic*.

But the zone we most want to occupy – and where our employers want us to be too – is *impact*. Here we can be productive, actively engaged and strategic.

The chaos of the B-Suite

A Harvard Business Review study found that in the 1970s executives received about 1,000 messages per year. In the 2010s they received around 30,000 per year (Folkman, 2015).

You do the math for today. We are so busy our eyes are watering.

The speed of work expectations is picking up too — we need to move faster to keep up with the pace of work and stay ahead of our competition.

What a combination. Do more and do it faster. Too much to do and too little time.

Sound familiar?

- Doing more
- With less
- Priorities changing daily
- Organisational restructures every second Thursday
- Can't answer half the questions your teams are asking
- Just as surprised as they are by major announcements
- The boss keeps changing direction
- No clear line of sight between corporate strategy and your day-to-day decisions
- Less airtime than ever with your boss.

Many of today's B-Suite leaders live in a world that is hyper fast-paced. Doing a lot more with a lot less, feeling stretched thin and barely balancing the chaos is a typical day in the office for a modern-day leader. They can't remember a day when they were not busy. They can't remember when a plan did exactly what it said it would do on the day. They can't remember when things ran like clockwork. All they know is fast-paced, busy and changeable.

> Doing a lot more with a lot less, feeling stretched thin and barely balancing the chaos is a typical day in the office for a modern-day leader.

The disempowerment of the B-Suite

Leadership in the B-Suite is a tricky game, and the pathway to the top is unclear, highly changeable and full of pitfalls. You're constantly second-guessing and translating what the C-level Executives are looking for. That's because you're often too junior to be in the room, yet senior enough to be looked up to by your team and expected to provide information, decisions, direction and confidence when you typically have very little to go on.

Disempowered leadership is the lack of autonomy and the illusion of authority.

On the odd day, when the pace drops off for a moment, B-Suite leaders notice how disempowered they feel. With little information flow from the top (and so much of it changeable and conflicting) it's sometimes hard to know where to turn your attention. What are the biggest priorities? Where's your biggest ROI? What's not going to change halfway through and negate all your effort? There is so much you could be doing with the downtime, but as you aren't close enough to the priorities to know where to focus, you aren't confident it wouldn't be a waste of time and energy.

Occupational health research quoted in a World Health Organization article stated that 'the most stressful type of work is that which values excessive demands and pressures ... where there is little opportunity to exercise any choice or control, and where there is little support from others' (Stavroula, 2003).

This disempowerment can be paralysing. Your confidence in what direction to take becomes shaky – there are so many options, which one is right? You know you don't have the authority to make a call, but equally, you don't have time to waste waiting for permission.

You might be forgiven for standing still, perhaps slowing down and waiting to see what happens tomorrow when the pace gets switched back on. But doing that doesn't make you happy. You don't like not knowing what to do. You don't like not having answers for your team, and you don't like being kept in the dark. Ultimately, you're feeling less powerful and less confident as a leader, and this gets worse, the longer it continues.

Fleeting moments of being strategic

We'd all like to be more strategic, but unless the word *strategy* is in your job title, you get little opportunity to focus there – no matter what level you're playing at. In an ideal world, we would reduce the pace of day-to-day work and create the space for strategy, but realistically this doesn't happen too often.

Strategy is the holy grail of leadership. We all want it, we all think someone else is doing it, but most of us haven't the time for it.

🔊 **strategy**

/ˈstratɪdʒi/

noun

1. a plan of action designed to achieve a long-term or overall aim.
   "time to develop a coherent economic strategy"

   Similar: master plan   grand design   game plan   plan of action   plan   ⌄

2. the art of planning and directing overall military operations and movements in a war or battle.
   "he was a genius when it came to military strategy"

   Similar: the art of war   military science   military tactics   generalship

Figure 2: Definition of strategy (Oxford Dictionary)

But that's the *planning* type of strategy – the first kind in the definition above – which sets a goal and describes how you're going to get there. Let's call this The Strategy. In corporates, it is often set from the top, on a one, three or five-year horizon. By the time it hits most B-Suite leadership scorecards, your direct connection to it has often become a little lost. Your goals and KPIs can feel forced to fit or even retro-fitted, and The Strategy has little or no bearing on your ability to continually reprioritise. It's too high level and often too set-and-forget. It's rarely a tool that adds value to your day-to-day leadership.

The second definition is less about formulating a long-term plan, and more about directing movement. Let's call this Being Strategic.

> In a world where all plans are subject to change, Being Strategic has become more valuable than The Strategy.

For me, this is strategy in action, and it's where the biggest impact happens. It's about being smart in the moment, making good decisions, making the right move and doing so quickly.

In a world where all plans are subject to change, Being Strategic has become more valuable than The Strategy.

And the great news is you can learn Being Strategic, and it levels up your leadership almost overnight.

Being Strategic is what we do when we are working on our leadership game – when we think like a fast-paced chess player. And Being Strategic can fit into our day-to-day approach with only a few minor adjustments. This book will show you how.

B-Suite leaders with impact

What's true of most B-Suite leadership roles, is that we are continually asked to do more with less.

With corporate restructures now an annual activity in most organisations, many B-Suite leaders face rolling change as a normal state of affairs. We are always on the back foot as productivity is constantly set back while workflows, relationships and ways of working are disrupted. Harvard Business Schools, Professor Rosabeth Moss Kanter, coined the term Kanter's Law, to explain that all change makes the situation worse before it can get better (Kanter, 2009). So in this cycle of constant change, we are permanently stuck in that valley of *worse* before we can reach the never-arriving peak of *better*.

In many cases, the expectations of our C-Suite seem to outstrip the reality when it comes to creating efficiency. Too often the B-Suite are left managing the gap that's left between what was expected and what actually happens. And with fewer resources in between.

B-Suite leaders carry the can of an ever-widening gap between top-line expectations and bottom-line reality.

We are left to close the gap ourselves; sometimes with our own bare hands, it feels. There is good reason that B-Suite leaders are experiencing burnout at rates never seen before.

In 2018, an international team of university-based researchers carried out a study of middle-managers. Their report described these managers as leaders who serve as an important connection between senior executives and frontline employees, yet are often sandwiched between these two groups. The researchers noted these middle managers experience demands and pressures from both sides, and as a result, high-stress levels and subsequent burnout are normal (Ahlvik, 2018).

Instead of burnout, we want to be able to operate like a C-Suite Executive – seemingly effortlessly handling the pace, using the space to think, and wielding the influence to assure outcomes.

That's the ultimate in high impact leadership, right?

The problem is that few firms are guiding their B-Suite to achieve C-level impact, so those leaders who can do it are standing out in the crowd. Learning to manage the pace so you can create the space to think is one of the most useful skills that any leader can master.

Knowing how to use that space to think clearly and to allow yourself to focus on influence rather than 'activity' really levels up our leadership game. It's what separates disempowered and chaotic leaders from impactful and strategic ones.

I know where you'd rather be – and that's really what Level Up is about.

Are you ready to level up? Are we on the same page about how you're feeling in the B-Suite? Do you recognise the importance of your role and how imperative it is that you learn to have greater influence, confidence and impact?

Good. First things first then – let's identify a few blockers that might be getting in your way and then we'll address them later in the book.

Influencing sucks

Wouldn't the job be so much easier if people just did what we wanted?

We all wish for more influence and wish that it was easier and less time consuming to exert.

But for many, the thought of deliberate influence is a bit unpleasant. Managing up is often confused with brown-nosing or climbing the greasy pole, and the art of influencing can sometimes feel manipulative or political. For many leaders, the idea of exerting influence brings images of sleazy salespeople, and they instinctively shy away.

> Managing up is often confused with brown-nosing or climbing the greasy pole, and the art of influencing can sometimes feel manipulative or political.

To make matters worse, we have a secret fear that putting ourselves out there opens us up for rejection. That if we ask for what we want, we may be told 'No'.

Many of us feel that we should *be* asked, rather than have *to* ask.

It's as though we want to *have* influence, but don't want to have to *exert* influence to get it.

'The key to successful leadership today is influence, not authority.'

– Ken Blanchard

Confidence is a sly fox

Confidence is mercurial, isn't it?

Some days we feel ten-feet-tall and bulletproof, while on others we undermine ourselves with self-doubt or second-guessing rather than pressing on.

Some days we are pumped for networking or public speaking, and other days we'd rather dig our eyeballs out with a spoon.

Some days we skip over corporate landmines whistling a happy tune, and other days we lose sleep, jump at shadows and see threats everywhere.

Most of the time we feel like we are winging it, like an imposter who's pretending they know what they're doing – when really they don't. We despise the idea of having to 'fake it till you make it', yet we do so most days. And all the while, a smug inner voice promises that any minute, someone will spot our deception.

Your reputation precedes you

Most of us shudder at the thought of self-promotion. We get cranky when our efforts are not recognised and infuriated to see someone else get credit unfairly. Somehow we believe that if we work hard and produce good work, then our work will speak for itself. Which it doesn't; our work doesn't have a voice.

Too many B-Suite leaders are neglecting their reputation. It's a classic example of failing to work *on* our business, and only working *in* our business. It's a mistake that C-Suite leaders don't make. We miss the fact that our reputation serves the team better than our hard work ever can – and that our reputation can be worth many times more than our personal contribution.

We want to be known, but we'd rather not say *look at me* to achieve it.

Leadership development isn't working

Leadership development outcomes, methods and competencies all need addressing to meet the needs of new business and new leaders.

From	To
Panicked	Well-paced
Paralysed	Productive
Powerless	Promotable

Table 1: Leadership development goals

We need to support B-Suite leaders to control the pace rather than feel panicked by it. To unlock their leadership, so they stop feeling paralysed and start being more productive regardless of circumstance. We need them to feel less powerless in the face of today's fast-paced and furious work so we can develop the B-Suite into a pipeline for promotion into the C-Suite.

Pace

We desperately need to keep pace with business shifts – current decision-making speeds and reaction-times are too slow for today's business needs. While some of this is structural and systematic in the form of approval processes and red tape, some relates to leadership agility. The 2018 Global Leadership forecast tells us that a leader's ability to react to high-speed change makes them 8.8 times more valuable to the business than a leader who can't (DDI, 2018).

Reacting – or Being Strategic is fast becoming more important than The Strategy. The pace and volatility of doing business mean reaction times are critical. B-Suite leaders who can operationalise rapidly, reset direction and make fast decisions are becoming increasingly prized. It seems that operational is no longer a dirty word – in fact, it's the embodiment of strategy in action.

> *'Without strategy, execution is aimless.*
> *Without execution, strategy is useless.'*
>
> – Morris Chang

Productivity

Increasingly important is a leader's ability to maintain their effectiveness despite the lack of predictability and constant change. The Global Leadership Forecast 2018 estimated that a leader who can set and reset direction and remain productive despite the chaos is worth almost twice one who can't.

Ambiguity is a major blow to productivity as we know it. B-Suite leaders everywhere are struggling to master ambiguity, to make decisions with incomplete information and act decisively despite uncertainty. The Forecast suggests that those who can, have more than three times the impact of those who cannot (DDI, 2018).

Promotability

Succession planning is going backwards. The Forecast reported that since 1999 there has been continued worldwide slippage in companies that feel they have a decent bench to replace those moving on or retiring. In 2018, only 31 per cent of Australian and New Zealand firms felt they had a strong bench. This lack of promotability in our leadership ranks is a major problem for employers and puts the business at risk (DDI, 2018).

In 2013 I developed one of the largest and most successful internal careers solutions in Australia, moving 10,000 people into new careers and roles instead of retrenching them. And in doing so, I learned a depressing truth. For most people, especially those in the B-Suite, the easiest way to their next career step is to leave and go to a new employer.

Internal career mobility is less successful than open market mobility because companies are increasingly inclined to hire managers from the outside rather than promote from within.

Doesn't it negate the effort we put into annual Talent Reviews if we are still not developing a successful pipeline of talent? Instead, we pay more for new hires (an internal promotion will typically cost organisations five to seven per cent in terms of salary increase, whereas an external hire will cost around 20 per cent). They take longer to perform in the role and are more likely to leave than someone who was promoted internally (Bersin, 2017).

But rather than rage against the machine, we need to help our B-Suite leaders to navigate it better. Once they become part of the furniture, they are at risk of being overlooked through systemic bias. Lacking the wow factor of a new hire, they tend to be judged by their failings more readily than their successes. It's something we blissfully overlook (or are ignorant of) with new hires. As a result, B-Suite leaders often fail to move from narrow functional leadership to operating in a more cross-functional, higher-impact capacity. Levelling up their impact would not only help them – it would be better for their employer as well.

Middle managers should be seen as a resource to be developed. They are literally the glue that holds an organisation together, without whom transformation, performance, culture and engagement would flounder. We must invest in them as a priority.

As Simon Sinek writes in *Start with Why*, 'Some in management positions operate as if they are in a tree of monkeys. They make sure that everyone at the top of the tree looking down sees only smiles. But all too often, those at the bottom looking up see only asses' (Sinek, 2009).

Training solutions are missing the mark

In terms of training, there's a mismatch between what B-Suite leaders want and what they get.

What they want is to learn from experienced peers and experts – just look at the dramatic rise in popularity of closed professional chat forums and peer networks. Look at the increasing levels of mentoring and coaching, and the value that B-Suite leaders place on having someone outside their organisation with the experience to give them objective, practical advice.

Yet organisations continue to invest in coaching-by-your-leader. While it certainly has value for on-the-job performance, it's problematic if you truly want to level up. Some leaders don't know how to help you operate at a different level (like my leader at the health fund). For them, it is mostly intuitive, and they struggle to pass it on. And some leaders don't want you to level up; you are too valuable to them exactly as you are. Most internally developed training programs are too generic to add real value to an experienced B-Suite leader. These commitments to in-house coaching and training mean there is minimal budget left for a B-Suite leader to explore the kinds of development that works for them, yet they are getting little value from what they do receive.

The Global Leadership Forecast mentioned earlier showed that the number one preference for high potential B-Suite leaders is external mentoring. Yet that doesn't even feature in the top five investments by organisations.

There's a frustrating mismatch between B-Suite needs and employer investment.

Millennials don't rate the training programs that their predecessors liked. Programs that the majority of Baby Boomers will report as excellent impress far fewer Millennials.

Organisations can't afford leadership training for B-Suiters – there are too many of them.

> Organisations can't afford leadership training for B-Suiters – there are too many of them.

Instead, significant training dollars are spent on a small selection of high performing or senior leaders, and proportionally little on the large number of middle managers in the B-Suite.

Most leaders have never had a mentor or coach, and the more junior the leader, the more likely this is to be so. Yet external coaching lowers leader turnover far more than coaching from managers.

Global Leadership Forecast 2018 data reveals that organisations that use coaching by direct managers and external mentors show greater leadership bench strength, promote more leaders from within, and are more likely to have a pipeline of talent to fill roles immediately.

B-Suite leaders need many skills

With the increasing pace of change comes greater complexity in determining which skills will best service leaders in the future. But if we tie our investment to our strategic challenges, then shaping B-Suite leaders to handle the pace better, deliver productivity despite the changing landscape and develop a strong bench of promotable candidates, seems like a safe bet.

Deloitte's 2019 human capital survey (Deloitte, 2019) tells us that the most critical competencies for 21st-century leadership are:

- leading through more complexity and ambiguity
- leading through influence
- leading more quickly.

Levelling up

The way we perform in the B-Suite has a significant impact on our seniority, but it is fluid, not fixed like a hierarchy. At times performance levels up, and at others, it slips back. But we typically occupy one mode about 80 per cent of the time, and that's where we want to level up to achieve our desired impact.

	Mode	Focus	Impact
Determines what work gets done	Executive	Vision	x 100
	Strategist	Ownership	x 50
	Influencer	Control	x 20
Determines how the work gets done	Innovator	Influence	x 6
	Process Owner	Expert	x 3
	Process Administrator	Trust	x 2

Table 2: Six modes of leadership

As the table above describes, the biggest shift is moving from being in charge of *how* the work gets done, to being in charge of *what* work gets done. It is the difference between working *in* your business versus working *on* your business.

To permanently level up how we operate and make the changes stick, we have to consciously challenge our training, mindset and beliefs.

'Efficiency is doing the thing right.
Effectiveness is doing the right thing.'

– Peter Drucker

A telling sign that you're operating in the top half of the frame is that you will be working across functions far more often than in your own function.

Let's unpack the modes in more detail.

Process Administrator

New leaders typically operate in Process Administrator mode. They are highly supervised (and initially grateful for it) and expected to execute everything precisely as instructed. Their world is one of learning to manage others and ensuring the quality and consistency of the function with which they are entrusted. A Process Administrator can quickly get frustrated if they are slow to be viewed as a trusted pair of hands and tasked with a little more autonomy to own the process rather than simply administer it.

Sam is our Process Administrator. She's recently been promoted, taking a step up from high performer to team leader. Sam is worried that she won't be able to add value to her peers. She hasn't led a team before and is painfully aware that she doesn't know what she's doing. Sam's doing her best to hide her insecurities from her team and her boss, and is working hard to earn their trust as a leader.

Process Owner

In Process Owner mode, you're trusted to both lead your team and to manage the process within certain boundaries. But perhaps you feel taken for granted at times. Your success in achieving operational excellence is not as highly regarded as you would like, and you want to be seen as an expert in your space – the go-to person in your company.

Julian is our Process Owner – he's ultimately responsible for the performance of a process or service. He spends significant time assessing where there is room for improvement and training his team to apply themselves to a consistently high standard.

Julian loves his job and feels he has stepped up as a people leader this year. But it's starting to annoy him that his manager is still making his people and process decisions. It makes him feel a bit redundant – just a middle man.

He's keen to establish himself as the expert in the eyes of his manager and to be given more leeway to make decisions in his space. He says that she doesn't want to relinquish control, but privately he's worried that she doesn't trust him.

Innovator

Those in the B-Suite feel they are often in Innovator mode – as recognised experts, given autonomy and control over the work and established as a people leader. But while the Innovator has high levels of freedom, it is often the most frustrating level, as you feel you've reached a pinnacle of mastering *how* the work gets done, only to recognise that you want more control over determining *what* gets done. The Innovator's primary focus and frustration is the lack of influence beyond their function. Their impact is important but limited by this constraint.

'The value of an idea lies in the using of it.'

– Thomas Edison.

Marina is our Innovator. She leads a modest function, is the company's recognised expert in her subject matter, and is known for having smart ideas and implementing them well. As a result, Marina has great autonomy to get the work done.

She's fought hard to establish her reputation as an expert solution-provider, developed a close-knit, high-performing team, and battled for the budget that she uses frugally to hone the function's performance to perfection.

Marina should be enjoying the fruits of her labour, but instead, she is frustrated. She isn't getting heard further up the chain, and she's not gaining traction with the other functional leaders who impact on her area. That Subject Matter Expert label she worked so hard to establish has now become a pigeonhole.

For Marina, influence is everything. Learning to manage up and across is key to leveraging her functional expert status and starting to craft a reputation as an influencer of larger, more complex solutions.

Influencer

Influencers are great agitators and advisors; they ask the right questions and surface the right issues to start the right cross-functional conversations. Often frustrated by a lack of control over the outcomes of these conversations, the Influencer makes a name for themselves outside the remit of their own function. Having an impact that exceeds their role boundary, the Influencer has learned to control the pace, giving them enough room to operate more strategically. They are adept at influencing conversations but not yet outcomes, and they want to exert more direct control over those.

*Temitope Ibrahim, wrote that 'Influence is
when you are not the one talking, and yet
your words fill the room; when you are absent
and yet your presence is felt everywhere'*
– (Ibrahim, 2017).

Christine is our Influencer. She knows that the greatest impact she can have for her team is to focus on influencing outcomes rather than managing her people. Her peers are beginning to trust her intent and collaborate more openly now – but it wasn't that easy at the beginning.

Christine's skills are in asking the right questions and bringing attention to the right issues, but she's a little frustrated by the time and effort it takes to rally others around the solution. Getting and keeping buy-in is time-consuming and exhausting, and sometimes she feels that there's nothing but her determination keeping these cross-functional collaborations going.

Christine wants to establish more control over these complex outcomes but isn't sure how to do so.

Strategist

Some of us are here – operating in Strategist mode. Recognised not only for our ability to ask the right questions and gain buy-in, but for being able to design, lead and deliver large, complex and politically nuanced projects and solutions. The Strategist has learned to think clearly and strategically, and to exert influence, but is often missing a sense of ownership. They are indispensable to more senior executives as a trusted advisor and create significant impact for their business, but don't have the ultimate accountability for which they yearn.

'A vision without a strategy remains an illusion.'
— Lee Bolman, Author, *Reframing the Path to School Leadership: A Guide for Principals and Teachers*

Vince has been a Strategist for ages. The trusted adviser to his C-level Executive, he is masterful at influencing leaders to think strategically, asking the right questions, leveraging his networks to knit together cross-functional collaborations and even arbitrating conflicting agendas to drive the outcomes that his Exec relies so much on him to deliver. But he wants more.

Vince wants ownership. A chance to prove to himself that he can take ultimate responsibility with success.

On the surface, he's afraid he's too useful to let go. While his Executive knows his desire to take that final step up, Vince is concerned that the timing will never be right for her to do without him. Privately, Vince is afraid he's not enough of an expert to win the respect of a big team and, having never managed a P&L before; he is unsure whether he understands what ultimate responsibility looks like.

Vince feels precarious. He knows what a valuable spot he holds in being indispensable to his Executive. What if he loses her trust in this venture? If he fails in his Executive bid, does he also risk his current hard-earned spot as her trusted lieutenant?

Executive

This level is where we most want to operate as here we are influential, confident and easily recognised. These leaders find themselves influencing outcomes fluently, thinking clearly and strategically, and determining direction with confidence. Executive mode raises your impact in the company, which of course boosts your career. Because influencing, thinking and decision-making come more easily, they can focus on their vision for the future and leading others to that place.

Ann leads a business of more than 3,000 employees and is accountable for almost 50 per cent of her organisation's revenue. She is confident, clear-headed, and a natural influencer who networks well, manages her CEO and Board extremely successfully and has great staff engagement. Before she levelled up, Ann would second guess her decisions, fail to delegate consistently and strategically, and was on the verge of burning herself out.

By working through some of the tenets of Level Up, she was able to engage and empower her direct reports rapidly and safely, learned to harness her inner voice and to establish more robust decision-making criteria that she shared more easily with others. Her self-confidence lifted, and she empowered and engaged her teams to achieve more together. Ann gave herself much-needed space to think so she could operate consistently like a C-Suite leader – a level she soon achieved.

It's a game of snakes and ladders

Your operating level is fluid: it's affected by your personal capabilities but also by external factors such as company culture and the expectations that others, especially the C-Suite, have on

> An Executive who expects more will give you greater room to grow than one who expects less of you.

your role. These act like the snakes and ladders of a childhood game, presenting opportunities to accelerate your operating level or have it slide frustratingly backwards.

These opportunities are readily apparent when you change employers. When the cultural norms and executive expectations on your role are different, they might expect more, allowing you to lift up, or they might expect less, which can be a constraint. When you're looking to level up inside your organisation, it's especially important to identify these nuances. An Executive who expects more will give you greater room to grow than one who expects less of you. It's an important strategy to learn when shaping a career within your existing organisation. You must be ready to seize – or avoid – these rare chances for reinvention.

When heading up an essential function at her large and complex employer, Sally feared she had become part of the furniture. Operating as an Innovator, she was the resident expert leading a well-oiled function, yet she felt invisible. Her executive stakeholders were no longer paying any attention, and it appeared she was doing her job too well. Sally had tried explaining her situation but got an 'If it ain't broke, don't fix it' response.

Sally's external factors shifted with the arrival of a new Executive who brought a different view of her function. He expected more and so she delivered, illustrating to other executives what they should have been asking from her all along. This new Executive's expectation was a snakes and ladders moment that enabled her to level up her leadership.

Which level are you at?

By now you should be clear about where you currently play and the mode you'd prefer to play at. Complete the following self-assessment, and then, based on the section where your answers scored highest, go to the sections that are of most interest. That's where you'll find the actions that are most relevant for you right now. These will help you increase your influence and impact.

Or, just read the book from front to back! It's up to you.

Use the following scale to rate yourself in each area:

1. I'm nowhere near it
2. I'm getting there
3. I'm doing well
4. I'm nailing it

CONTROL THE PACE				
I can make clear, confident decisions under pressure.	1	2	3	4
I am comfortable with ambiguity and typically make good decisions with incomplete information.	1	2	3	4
I am good at bringing the right people together to problem-solve complicated issues pretty quickly.	1	2	3	4
I am confident to take action even when I am uncertain about the right one.	1	2	3	4
I can handle disruptions fluidly and reprioritise quickly, seamlessly and confidently.	1	2	3	4
I'm able to ensure my team has the space to innovate.	1	2	3	4
I'm known for being productive and not flustered.	1	2	3	4

USE THE PACE				
I'm managing the pace of work so I can make space to think.	1	2	3	4
I'm good at strategic thinking and problem-solving.	1	2	3	4
I have a consistent and logical approach to making quality decisions under pressure.	1	2	3	4
I have a clear view of the best way to frame complex problems and rarely find myself approaching them in the wrong way, causing rework for myself and my team.	1	2	3	4
I have a good handle on my confidence, and rarely second guess myself, even in private.	1	2	3	4
I'm able to ensure my team has the space to innovate.	1	2	3	4
I'm known for moving fast but thoughtfully.	1	2	3	4
MAKE THE CASE				
I'm good at managing up, and my leaders appreciate it.	1	2	3	4
I'm comfortable with my level of influence outside my direct function.	1	2	3	4
I make time to think about my influencing approach.	1	2	3	4
I rarely have business cases knocked back by my Executive.	1	2	3	4
I am conscious of the impact of my leadership brand and actively manage my reputation internally (and externally).	1	2	3	4
I have a reputation for achieving great results through organising and motivating cross-functional collaboration – even when it is hard.	1	2	3	4
My team and I have a reputation for high performance.	1	2	3	4

Table 3: **Leadership level diagnostic**

Leading in the B-Suite can feel like being a giant umbrella, shielding those below from those above, so your team can get on with important work without all the noise. We absorb that noise, filter out the distractions, piece information together to work out what's happening and then project confidence and certainty to those around us – even when we are feeling anything but!

B-Suite leaders are always looking for new ways to manage the relentless pace of work and new ways to cope with the chaos. They want space to think, and the skills to think well. And they want to exert influence effectively, so it becomes second nature to them.

That's why I designed the Level Up program to focus on the three principles that are essential for B-Suite managers.

Leading in the B-Suite can feel like being a giant umbrella, shielding those below from those above, so your team can get on with important work without all the noise.

PART TWO
SO WHAT,
NOW WHAT?

'I never dreamed about success. I worked for it.'

– Estée Lauder

Three principles

As leadership coach and author Marshall Goldsmith said, 'The only thing I don't think people understand about good leaders is that they're both good and lucky. A lot of it is timing' (Goldsmith, n.d.).

Making an impact in the B-Suite is not just luck, it's about strategically using approaches that make all the difference. The luck I'll leave to you – but put in the work, and you'll be surprised how much luckier you get.

In Part Two we'll explore the three principles required to level up your leadership, and unpack ten practical strategies to do so.

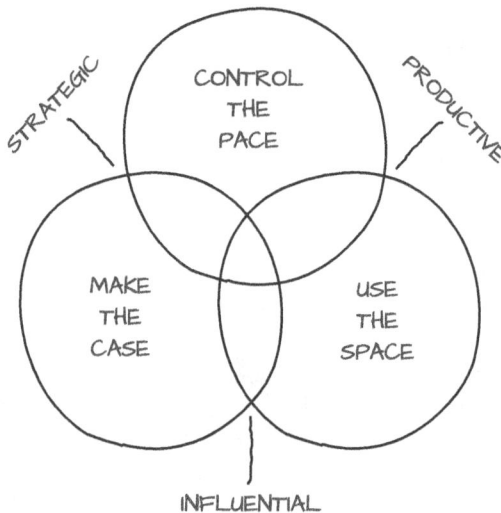

Figure 3: Level Up key principles

1. Control the pace

Work is beyond frantic, and we are desperate to get organised, manage conflicting and ever-changing priorities, make decisions and generally get some semblance of order in place for our teams as well as our sanity. In this section of the book, we'll explore tactics to get a better handle on the frantic pace of work – to control the pace and create a bit of space to think.

The ability to control the pace and use the space to think means that you are more readily able to turn strategy into action, and to be strategic every day. This creates more autonomy for you and impact for your teams.

2. Use the space

I hear a lot of B-Suite leaders bemoaning their lack of time to do strategic work. But few of us are taught to think strategically, so even with all the time in the world, we may not know where to start. The chances are we would still bury ourselves in busy work and complain we don't have time. This section will show you how to be strategic in bite-sized bits of space carved out from your busy day.

Being able to right-size the balance between controlling the pace and making the case is essential to you being able to right-size your productivity – to manage both the work and the expectations of others with greater ease.

3. Make the case

Being able to make a compelling case for your senior leaders, your peers or your teams is an essential element of success in the

B-Suite. Making a compelling case is essential to leadership, and being skilled at it enables you to operate at a totally different level. Many B-Suite leaders assume that it comes naturally to some and not to others. Yet it is a highly learnable skill and therefore, more accessible and attainable than it appears. This section will provide insight into the skills you can practise to manage up, manage out and manage outcomes, and the three directions where making the case is key to success.

Using the space to ensure that you're making the case where it matters most is a fast way to increasing your influence in your organisation.

Control the Pace

'Focus on being productive, instead of busy.'

– Tim Ferris

In the Levelling Up section, we examined six different modes of leadership, recognising the lower levels can feel as though we have no influence over what work gets done. That puts us at the mercy of more work being thrown our way with less clarity on how to prioritise it all.

The danger is that it impacts our productivity – we either get buried in work, work on the wrong things, or make wrong decisions in relation to managing the work. Getting this balance right is crucial for productivity.

As work becomes increasingly overwhelming, learning how to strategically manage the pace of your work has become a key survival skill. So we start here to safeguard many B-Suite leaders from the very real prospect of burnout.

The stronger our operating mode, the more we can do to control the pace – instead of letting it control us.

This section covers four steps for controlling the pace of work:

1. Coping
2. Prioritising
3. Planning
4. Deciding

Why control the pace of work?

When you're in the B-Suite, you don't have time to breathe, let alone think. You're being pulled down into the detail of managing your team and their work, pulled sideways into complex collaboration and supporting your team's success from outside your function, and pulled up into committees, papers and board preparation.

It's no surprise that more than 70 per cent of leaders sometimes feel they are at burnout (Stavroula, 2003).

In 1981, Christine Maslach and Susan Jackson published the Maslach Burnout Inventory, a psychological test measuring an individual's experience of burnout across three key dimensions.

If you recognise yourself in one of the following, then that 70 per cent of leaders might include you:

Exhaustion. Are you experiencing a sense of ongoing, pervasive tiredness and lethargy that is the opposite to the high-energy go-getter you usually consider yourself to be?

Feelings of cynicism or detachment. When with someone you trust – a friend, partner or mentor – do you sometimes share that you wonder if work is worth it? Do you ever feel that your commitment and loyalty go unnoticed and wonder why you bother?

Sense of professional ineffectiveness and lack of accomplishment. Do you have quiet concerns that you are failing? That you are not up to the mark? That you are making mistakes that another, better person would not? Do you feel like it's Groundhog Day where nothing you do seems to make any difference? Do you sometimes think there's a growing gap between how hard you are working and how well it is working (Maslach, 1981)?

Guilt is an area I believe is missing from the Maslach Inventory. It is the emotional discomfort that arises when you feel responsible for something that offended or hurt someone else. It's made even worse in the leadership context when it comes from something you feel should be in your control yet isn't – such as setting a direction for the team with insufficient information, or not having adequate resources to match the workload.

Naturally, we worry that team members are suffering as much as we are, and feel responsible for that suffering – and we suspect (or perhaps know) that they hold us accountable for it too. And even though we recognise that, as a B-Suite leader, there is a limited amount we can do about it, we still allow ourselves to be impacted by guilt.

If you're a B-Suite leader, I'd be surprised if you haven't felt at least some of these things.

Burnout is a risk when the demands of a job outstrip a person's ability to cope with the stress.

In B-Suite leadership, key drivers of stress are everywhere – changeable deadlines, conflicting agendas and demands, long working hours, ambiguity around status, uncertainty of direction and lack of autonomy. Richard Gunderman is quoted as describing this stress as 'the accumulation of hundreds or thousands of tiny disappointments, each one hardly noticeable on its own' (Deligkaris, 2014). So why, apart from feeling tired, detached and somewhat failing (as if that wasn't enough) does this matter?

Why does it matter, and matter now?

Onset burnout is a self-fulfilling prophecy. Evidence suggests that long-term stressors make you less effective. You know that creeping feeling of failure? The longer you let it linger, the more likely it is to come true.

A study based on students showed that attention, memory and cognitive functioning are all impaired when you're under prolonged pressure – at risk of burning out (Deligkaris, 2014). But this was only based on the accumulated stress of four weeks of exam preparation, not several years of the accumulated stress of managing the madness of the B-Suite!

> The pace of change has never been this fast, and it will never be this slow again.

At the 2018 World Economic Forum, Canadian Prime Minister Justin Trudeau commented, 'The pace of change has never been this fast, and it will never be this slow again.' And he's right. The pace of work is picking up. But it's more than just speed that's making it crazy.

It's also more complicated, uncertain, inter-related and changeable than it's ever been. The frequency of altered plans, changed goals and derailed direction is bewildering. It would be understandable if you felt that all your hard work was not working. But it doesn't feel that way.

Your performance is directly affected when you can't control the pace, so this is a critical place to start.

Coping

> *'If don't like something, change it. If you can't change it, change your attitude.'*
>
> – Maya Angelou

The need to exert control over difficult or complicated circumstances is a strong driver in most B-Suite leaders. We've got to where we are mainly by controlling our surroundings. But when a growing sense of being out of control stresses us out; we fight harder to exert control. Overwhelm sets in with too many plates spinning, too many balls juggling, and too many whistles blowing. And so we try even harder. It's a vicious circle.

We worry more – a lot more. With our amygdala in override mode, it's not necessarily logical, and sometimes we can't even put our finger on why. We worry about everything – large or small, urgent or not, close to home and far away. It's our subconscious seeking to assert control.

We seek to assert control consciously by micro-managing people – demanding that all contact comes through us or all decisions come across our desk for sign off. The less control we feel, the more we grip tighter. Yet the tighter we grip, the more things slip through our fingers. We can't be everywhere at once, so we become a bottleneck for our teams, and drown in our workload. The irony is that some of that workload was generated by asserting this level of control.

Unfortunately, our obsession with control is based on an illusion. When work was predictable and controllable, control was a highly prized leadership trait. Now it's an out of date concept – another holy grail.

> Our obsession with control is based on an illusion.

This myth that control is achievable and desirable is the first thing that undermines our coping mechanisms. In our brain, not being in control means we are not coping. That erodes our confidence and further damages our coping mechanisms.

So the first step is to stop this crippling mindset and reject this out of date concept. Control is an illusion – we have to learn to let go, surrender and go with the flow – but do so safely and productively.

Amanda was running a large team with multiple high priority projects and priorities. When her business merged with another, and her responsibilities doubled overnight, Amanda struggled to cope with the expanded role. Her reaction was to hold tighter to control; she insisted on gatekeeping communication to her team and making the big decisions, which meant she had to be at key meetings. The impact was a bottleneck on her team, increasing isolation from her business and an untenable workload. Yet the worse this got, the more Amanda tightened her grip. She was not coping.

Amanda and I worked hard on how she could cope with the workload and reduce her desire to control it all. We created a model that she could use to compartmentalise how she felt every time she felt out of control.

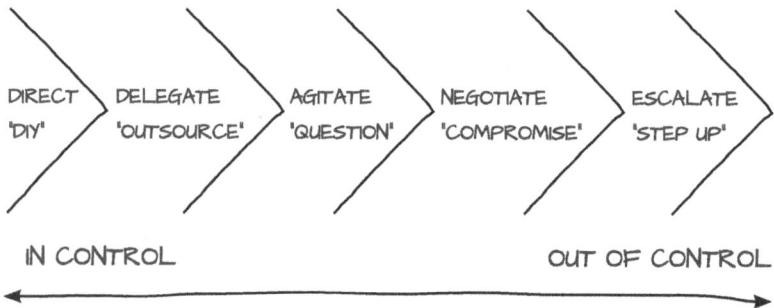

DIRECT 'DIY'   DELEGATE 'OUTSOURCE'   AGITATE 'QUESTION'   NEGOTIATE 'COMPROMISE'   ESCALATE 'STEP UP'

IN CONTROL   OUT OF CONTROL

Figure 4: Amanda's coping mechanism

Here's how to create a working model for yourself.

In no particular order, make a list of everything you are worried about – everything that feels out of control, or where you know you are over-controlling but can't help yourself. Sometimes you know others don't like it, but you can't see another option.

Don't spend a week on this; you'll probably get most things down in a couple of days. It's a dynamic tool, so add new items and remove others as you go.

Now group your concerns into the five sections.

1. Direct control (the Do It Yourself list): What can you control directly, without depending on anyone or anything else – such as your team, your leader or another peer or corporate process? This list is smaller than you think.

    The things that live here are niggling worries and tasks you can address with minimal intellectual effort and little risk of derailment. Doing the dishes, clearing out your inbox or submitting your tax return might not sound sexy, but it's the kind of thing that keeps you up at night and is mentally easy to tackle without outside help.

    Top tip: Do these tasks when your energy levels are low. This is mentally undemanding work that gives the same sense of completion-satisfaction as anything else on your list. These are your quick wins and easy rewards.

2. Delegate or Outsource: What do you have significant, but not complete control over? Typically, these rest in your direct lines of authority, such as your in-silo team activities or simple tasks or projects that require little interaction and don't depend on others.

    Top tip: Be clear about which tasks you will delegate – these are typically low complexity and low risk, and any failure is contained. They are a safe way to empower your direct reports without triggering an illusion of control meltdown for you. The clearer you are on the criteria for these tasks, the faster you'll outsource them when they appear. If there is a list in this section, it's purely so you can remember to check in with your delegatees.

3. Agitate or Question: Which items do you have little control over, but can influence? They include collaborative exercises, complex cross-functional projects or day-to-day interactions with other parts of the business – particularly those that impact on your team from the outside.

   Top tip: This is where a well-placed question can send others off to solve something that's impacting you. You don't have to address it directly, you just need others to see what you see so that they can fix it.

4. Negotiate or Compromise: Which tasks are bigger than you or your team? These are where you need to ask for help or open a dialogue about how to work together on a shared issue.

   Top tip: Rather than wonder 'how do I solve this?' think about which conversation is needed and with whom. It's more like 'How do I engage around this?'. See the win/win section of Make the Case later for more tips on how to do this.

5. The final section contains everything over which you have no control and very little influence, such as corporate strategy setting, corporate restructures, or external market forces.

Top tip: Make sure your opinions are heard, constructively, ahead of schedule. Ensure you have made the case with your Executive, but then walk away. When decisions are made without you, your job shifts from influencing the decision to working on its execution. Accept the decision with grace – even if it's hard. It was just as hard for them to make it and now we've just got to work with it. You're not going to change the decisions, but you can influence how you and your business respond to it, and work around not against it.

The game with this model is to make it dynamic. By applying the right tactics to the right items, we not only create an illusion of control (which stabilises that sense of feeling overwhelmed) we also portray the illusion of control (no matter what it is, we always seem to know exactly what to do.)

> Make sure your opinions are heard, constructively, ahead of schedule.

Both Bill Gates and Jeff Bezos do the dishes every night. Why? It allows them to work in their DIY space, doing something small and simple, which puts their other worries into perspective and recharges their batteries. It turns out they are both smart to do this (we did know they were smart, right?); a 2014 study in mindfulness determined that washing dishes for only six minutes can increase your sense of inspiration by 25 per cent and decrease your anxiety by 27 per cent (Hanley, 2014).

Prioritising

> *'The key is not to prioritise what's on your schedule, but to schedule your priorities.'*
>
> – Stephen Covey

This is the art of constantly adjusting what needs to be done, so you have the right people working on the right thing at the right time – all the time.

For high performing and transformative leaders, the act of prioritising is so ingrained in their minds and ways of working, that they don't even notice they are doing it. For the rest of us, it's a learnable habit and one I cannot recommend highly enough.

Almost all my Level Up clients have benefitted from this model at some stage in their journey. But they often hesitate to try it, instead using excuses such as the following.

I'm too busy...

It feels like an enormous task to evaluate what work is happening, what should be happening and who should be doing it, but it's only about an hour's work. Not doing it will mean that your 'too busy' will never change. Control the Pace!

I don't have The Strategy to anchor from...

It's helpful if you've got a corporate or divisional strategy that provides clear handrails for prioritising and decision-making. Most of the time The Strategy doesn't do that for us, and we have to make our own.

We never say no or stop things, so there's no point prioritising...

It's the other way around. You never say no or stop things because you have no prioritising framework. This framework, well communicated, is your best way to say no, not yet, or stop doing things in a way that is objective, consistent and strategic. Without a prioritisation framework, you are at the mercy of other people's priorities, and that makes you feel (and operate) like an order-taker, sliding down the leadership modes like snakes and ladders.

> Without a prioritisation framework, you are at the mercy of other people's priorities.

The gap between strategy and action can sometimes be so large that I fail to see the connection between what gets done on the front line and The Strategy, which was set in an executive offsite. Managers blame strategists for not providing clear enough guidelines for implementation. Strategists blame managers for not Being Strategic enough.

From my coaching experience, I know that while many people have heard of the most common prioritisation matrix – Eisenhower's Urgent versus Important matrix – few people actively use it to organise their workload. If you need a reminder to actually use it (and consider this a sharp reminder, a literal nudge in the ribs), I've added a quick explanation to the bottom of this section.

If you're a relative master at urgent versus important, then it's time to develop your own strategic prioritisation framework.

Being strategic eats The Strategy for breakfast

Strategic prioritisation frameworks are the secret weapon of leaders who manage the pace and create the space — both for themselves and for their teams. Using this approach *regularly* will help you to:

- Translate strategy into action rapidly and accurately
- Allocate resources intelligently and fluidly
- Objectively negotiate with conflicting priorities
- Engage others in your prioritising, so they understand where they sit and why.

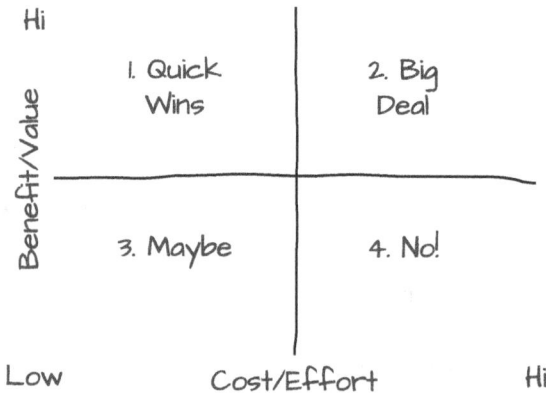

Figure 5: Strategic Prioritisation example

Every strategic prioritisation framework is different — the definitions that you choose for your axis are unique to your team and your organisation.

- The benefit/value is easiest to establish when anchored off a good corporate or divisional strategy. If you're in a big business, and you don't have a divisional strategy to close the gap between what you do and what The Strategy says, then you may find it easier to talk to your stakeholders about what their biggest value drivers are right now. Ask what would matter most to them that you can deliver. Depending on your business, these might include revenue, cost avoidance, efficiency, capability or growth. Find three or four definitions of value, so you have a clear sliding scale to prioritise against.

- You can articulate the cost/effort axis within your team. It can be estimated in labour hours, length of time or scale of complexity (often all three). Again, simply decide on a definition that suits you – for example a scale of 1-3 on each of those three criteria is an easy way to consistently and objectively place items where they belong along the X-axis.

Each of the four categories should be considered a category for tactics – this will help you to determine the priority of the work, and who should be working on it and most importantly – how to handle it.

In Figure 5, **Category One** means Quick Wins. These items allow you to create significant value and impact in a short period with minimum effort. This is where you win hearts and minds, and build a reputation for moving quickly, mobilising accurately and delivering high impact results. Make sure you produce outcomes from this category regularly. Put your fastest, most high energy leaders in here, and they will thrive on kicking golden goals for the team. Those who are more meticulous could cost you an opportunity to impress, so pick your people carefully. This is also a great category from which to gift your team a quick win from time to time – to keep them motivated and recognised at regular intervals.

Category Two is what I consider your Big Deals. This is high value, higher effort work; classically the bigger projects that an organisation has to tackle, such as a systems implementation or a new product or service. If you have too many of these on at once, your team's resources will be tied up in long-range deliverables. When I'm asked to help a team to reprioritise to cope with the workload, this is often the most congested area – everything they are doing is high value and high effort. This is draining on the team, who get little light relief or regular recognition. It's also a risk to your reputation as it leaves you with long windows of alleged inactivity (you're busy behind the scenes, but you haven't had a win in a while). And in corporations with notoriously short memories, it's a great idea to balance Categories One and Two carefully and deliberately. My advice is to delegate your best problem-solving brains and your most meticulous workers to Category Two and then to take a governance role yourself. Don't go in as the chief problem-solver – you'll be sucked into it permanently.

Category Three holds the Maybes. This is the list that you'll get to when you get the chance – the projects that you hold over for periods when the team is less busy. These low value and low complexity items are often of high value to your team (a back-office clear-out or a passion project), but not of strategic value beyond that. Evaluate these carefully as they can be really distracting. Can you move this up to a Category One or Two? Is it a useful back-office piece that will enable the team to be more efficient, in which case could you blitz it with an 'all hands on deck' approach over a couple of days for a Quick Win? Or is it lacking strategic weight; and would it benefit from finding a partnership to increase the value and impact that would push it up into a Big Deal? In my experience, use Category Three as a holding bay for things you are about to prioritise – otherwise they tend to fester there, untouched for months. Alternatively, gift it to a team-mate keen to cut their teeth on something or to have more autonomy. If you think any mistakes are easily contained, then this is a great on-the-job development opportunity you don't need to be too hands on with. A possible win/win.

Category Four is a straight-out no. Get out of there. This quadrant is dangerous for you and your team. You'll spend a lot of time and effort on something that won't be worth it, and you'll miss opportunities for Quick Wins along the way. Most organisations are resistant to cancelling priorities, citing sunk costs, but that's exactly what I recommend you consider. Especially if you can't make projects in this quadrant more valuable (turn them into Big Deals), or easier to deliver (which moves them into the Maybes).

> Most organisations are resistant to cancelling priorities, citing sunk costs, but that's exactly what I recommend you consider.

Use your model to manage expectations

Once you have this up and running and you're comfortable with your criteria and your tactics, share this with your collaborators, stakeholders and client groups. The sharing is important – it not only helps you test your prioritisation but provides a clear indication to your peers that you may be de-prioritising too. Once this is commonly understood and used consistently, you have created a platform for objective conversations about the work you are and are not doing.

Maria created her Strategic Prioritisation framework with clear and agreed definitions and was almost immediately able to manage expectations far more clearly and objectively with her stakeholders. 'I found that if I could show a stakeholder that their project was low value compared to others, or very complex to deliver, it became so much easier to negotiate expectations, resources and timeframes.'

She had developed a framework for negotiation with her stakeholders. They could partner with another project to increase their value and move into a Category One or Two. They could negotiate their expectations (reduce the complexity or timeframe) to move into Category One, or they could add in resources to reduce the level of effort associated.

> By designing, testing and then applying your own strategic prioritisation framework, you'll create a common set of handrails for your team to operate within.

By designing, testing and then applying your own strategic prioritisation framework, you'll create a common set of handrails for your team to operate within. You'll have more balance in terms of what work is being done – and more balance around who is best suited to what kind of pace. Your goal is to keep Category One closing out items regularly to create space for new ones. Keep Category Two low in volume so they can concentrate without distraction. Manage the conversation around the items in Category Three, so they are ready for promotion to One or Two when the time is right, and to manage expectations around Category Four – which means saying no with confidence.

Figure 6: Eisenhower matrix

Urgent versus important

For those of you who will benefit from a reminder about the Urgent versus Important matrix, here is how it works. I often find that using both frameworks helps me to juggle the priorities and helps my team to cope with the workload. The Eisenhower is a great individual prioritisation tool. If you replace your linear to-do list with a matrix, you'll find yourself becoming more productive fairly easily. It's a super-easy model to share with your team to help improve their ability to prioritise their time too.

'Doing something unimportant well does not make it important.'
Tim Ferriss

Many of my clients have theirs visible on a wall somewhere (physical or virtual). They use it to frame regular conversations with the team on what the work looks like, how the balance is going and what you — as their leader — need to be doing to help everything run smoothly.

Quadrant One is Do Now. If it's urgent and important, do it and do it right now. These are typically emergencies and hard deadlines, the things you stop other stuff for. If you've got loads in this area, then ask yourself if it is truly urgent and important, or do you just feel as if everything lives there at the moment? Check your perspective; do those tasks belong there compared to everything else or are you just panicking? If you are right and everything in there is truly urgent and important, call your boss. You want that square down to one or two tasks as quickly as possible, and that may mean you need help to ease the bottleneck.

Quadrant Two is Do Next. If it's important but not urgent, it doesn't have a pressing deadline, but it is important to your success. Practise deliberate procrastination with these, but watch your deadlines. Be disciplined, or they will become a level one task all too quickly.

Quadrant Three is Do Last. This is a space-maker, so use it. These tasks are not critical to your success, and nor are they urgent. If they are critical to someone else, consider delegating the task and upskilling a member of your team at the same time. If there is no-one dependent on this task, deprioritise it and get it off your list.

Quadrant Four means Do Never: What are you even doing with tasks in here? Get these items off the list now; they are taking up valuable space.

Planning

Whatever their leadership mode, many of my coaching clients find they have unexpectedly entered a bit of a slump. They know the world has changed, and they are looking for new toolkits to adapt, yet it's hard to pinpoint the tools that need to change and which can remain the same.

This can quickly turn into a productivity slump, which impacts both our teams and ourselves. Analyst, Josh Bersin, says that after every major revolution, there is a productivity slump as we re-learn how to operate (Bersin, 2017). And of course, we are in such a situation right now, with Industry 4.0.

The way we made plans and made decisions in the past can undermine how we operate today. It can paralyse us, set us up for disappointment and stop us from reacting quickly and nimbly when we need to.

What's changed?

Well, change has changed.

What used to be a straight line from here to there, is now about as linear as a bowl of spaghetti.

Australian change guru, Temre Green, once told me, 'Our reality is that the current state is in a state of flux, the future state is ambiguous, and the plan itself subject to change.' Boy did she sum that up perfectly!

Our current state is unknown. It is no longer the solid bedrock of certainty on which we used to operate. It's more interconnected and complex in its dependencies than ever, and that's why making decisions and changing things in isolation (in a silo) is becoming less viable and more likely to result in inadvertently impacting someone else's area.

Our future state is ambiguous – it's hard to see it clearly, or to know exactly where you will land. You may have a direction or a goal in mind, but like anyone who's navigated with only wind, waves and stars, your ability to land in one precise port is pretty slim.

And the plan is impossible to pin down. Have you noticed that planning cycles have shrunk from five years to three, and now to two-year plans? And most of these are done on a rolling annual basis, so really they are one-year plans, aren't they? The certainty horizon is getting shorter as disruption becomes more frequent.

It feels like navigating in a giant bowl of jello where nothing is solid.

What makes it more difficult is the tension within our brain between planning and deciding. When it comes to applying logic between the two, we are Jekyll and Hyde.

In our minds, plans are aspirational – full of options. To avoid making mistakes, we have to learn to examine those options through a risk lens before implementation and make sure we have a rigorous approach to developing them that manages our natural tendency to think our plans are great and will work.

In our minds, decisions are finite – the act of focussing on just one thing. The very etymology of 'decide' in Latin means to cut off something. Hailing from the same word family as regicide, suicide and homicide, decide literally means to kill off choices. The very opposite of planning, where we are full of options!

And this tension often catches us unaware, making our decision-making conservative when it needs to be experimental, and basing plans on optimism when they need to be based on risk.

So how do we set direction and achieve our goals in such a challenging landscape? Three strategies:

- Believe, and prepare for the reality that all plans are subject to change
- Plan to fail so every failure is a success
- Have big goals – be happier to come up short against a big goal than fully achieve a small one.

#allplansaresubjecttochange

Early on in our relationship, my husband would change our weekend plans at the last minute. It nearly broke us up – it was so damn irritating.

I'll let you into a little secret. I don't like my plans being spoiled. I don't like surprises, and I don't like being disrupted.

So every time I had a tantrum, he would say 'All plans are subject to change'. He says it so frequently, that now he even speaks the hashtag. 'HASHTAG all plans are subject to change.' So damn irritating.

But he's right – all plans are subject to change; and especially now. All plans are going to be detoured, derailed or disrupted no matter what you do.

59

Plan to fail

Do you know what's weird? Our brain actually sets our plans up to fail in the first place. It's not all about our environment. Our brain is so wildly optimistic about planning that Dan Kahneman has coined it 'The Planning Fallacy' (Kahneman, 2011).

Our tendency is to assume best-case outcomes, and to only consult the case studies of other successes. It's called reasoning by analogy — if it looks like project X it'll work like project X. Unfortunately all that glitters is not gold and suppressing reasonable doubts and neglecting ambiguous information means we are kidding ourselves with our best-laid plans.

Benjamin Franklin is reported to have said 'If you fail to plan, then you plan to fail.' But times have changed, and now planning to fail is a *good* thing.

Permission to fail is one thing, but limiting the fail by planning it carefully is a great thing. I'd update the President's famous quote to say 'have a plan to fail, but don't fail to plan'.

It's one thing to fail — but to plan for failure means the failure was planned. It's the difference between making a mistake, which is an uncontrolled failure and considering all the options for a controlled failure.

> Have a plan to fail, but don't fail to plan.

The great thing about a controlled failure is that the damage is controlled. The level of rework is limited, and the extraction of some value from the remains is highly likely. You may not have to start all over again because you planned to fail.

An uncontrolled failure means uncontrolled damage and often significant levels of rework with absolutely no prediction of how or why things went wrong.

This matters. We are in a world where mistakes are not ok, but a planned failure is celebrated. What matters is that you and your team emerge as adaptable, nimble and able to handle anything. And that reputation will take you places.

Anticipating and controlling failure is a major mindset shift for most managers.

Conduct a pre-mortem

Many leaders are familiar with the post-mortem, retrospective or project implement review that asks 'what went wrong?' This is useful, but I've often wondered if it isn't a bit late. While a valuable discipline, I'd rather you had identified (and avoided) it in the first place.

When establishing yourself as a leader who can control the pace, you will notice that you become someone who preempts and manages risks and is therefore prone to fewer mistakes.

We know that the human brain is inclined to being over-optimistic when it makes a plan. Our brains suppress doubt, and group-think pushes it away even more. Let's be honest; no-one wants to be the pessimist in the room. Most doubts get dismissed anyway, and we'd rather lead with optimism than caution any day of the week. The latter can be so *dull*.

We need to legitimise doubt without sucking the optimism from the room. The pre-mortem is a fun and creative way to instil a risk mindset without introducing pessimism into your culture.

Once you've completed your planning process, polish and perfect it with a simple question for your team:

> We need to legitimise doubt without sucking the optimism from the room.

What could possibly go wrong?

Let's pretend this was a disaster. What happened?

The important step is to get your team to write down their thoughts independently before they discuss it. This will let your introverts, pessimists and extroverts all shine equally without influencing each other, and avoid suppression of the doubts that you are looking to surface and plan for.

Have big goals

Does this mean that you can't have optimistic goals? No, not at all, in fact, quite the opposite. Bigger goals offer a more confident chance of extracting value from whatever happens because you have thought things through.

We've been trained to set realistic goals as leaders, and many of us were taught to under-promise and over-deliver. But McKinsey's research tells us that not setting audacious enough goals in the first place is one of the top three reasons for the failure of transformational leadership (Davies, et al., 2017).

So by sticking to this particular out-of-date-phrase, you are undermining yourself as a transformative leader.

Realistic goal: Put a man on the Moon. If the moon shot misses, we come back to earth empty-handed.

Level Up goal: Put a man on Mars. If the Mars shot misses, we'll probably land on the Moon on our way home.

Taking this approach of 'think big, hope for the best and plan for the worst' ensures that your team has options. Places where you can change direction, switch tactics and still land valuable outcomes.

Options are like the spare tire of leadership, and this approach will ensure that you have plenty.

Deciding

When work is this fast, complicated and changeable, decision-making is far more challenging. It's no wonder that B-Suite leaders come to me complaining of confidence issues and a sense of being paralysed by uncertainty.

Not long ago, the world of work was stable, predictable, routine and well defined. Now we look to B-Suite leaders to provide those elements, yet they are at the coal-face in a world of work that is anything but clear or consistent. It's an additional layer of pressure for B-Suite leaders to protect their teams from the chaos.

In a chaotic environment where we have too many choices, narrowing them down and eliminating some is crucial to carving a path forward. Yet leaders often receive increasing amounts of incomplete information, and in the end, the answer could be anything. Which all adds to the sense of overwhelm, and undermines our ability to cope.

I don't believe that we can simply learn to be comfortable in chaos. To thrive in chaos, we need to make sense of it. Our brains are wired to make sense of things, and even the most complex and changeable environments have patterns and tactics hidden inside.

> Our brains are wired to make sense of things, and even the most complex and changeable environments have patterns and tactics hidden inside.

As a headhunter in financial markets in London in the 1990s, I used to recruit quantitative analysts. Their value was finding predictable patterns in the chaos of the financial markets, and if they were good at it, they were worth many millions. My favourite source of top talent was chaos theorists from an astrophysics background, so I headhunted people from NASA to work for investment banks. If those people could find patterns in the stars and make sense of the universe, then I felt confident they could find and harness them in the chaos of work.

Leading in chaos requires the ability to:

1. Identify what kind of chaos you're experiencing (there are different categories)
2. Play to your strengths
3. Learn proven tactics with which to respond in all cases
4. Be adaptable (there will often be more than one thing going on)

Designed by the American military, the VUCA framework is an acronym for Volatility, Uncertainty, Complexity and Ambiguity. It is a great starting point for making sense and responding to the chaos of work. After all, if the military can invest billions in a methodology for leading in the chaos of combat, then the business world should pay attention. But VUCA doesn't always fit our context, so the model I work on with clients is VUCA-inspired but B-Suite specific.

Unpacking the categories of chaos

Volatility refers to the rate of change in an industry, market or the world in general. It is associated with fluctuations in demand, turbulence and speed, and is well-documented in the literature on industry dynamism. The more volatile the world, the faster and more frequently things change – and the higher the element of surprise. It's like an earthquake monitor, fluctuating up and down like crazy.

Uncertainty refers to the extent to which we can confidently predict the future. The more uncertain the world, the harder it is to predict. And this world has become so unpredictable that many experts are struggling to navigate it. Their knowledge and toolkits are being tossed aside by scenarios no-one has experienced before and situations that no-one could have statistically forecast or confidently predicted. It's not that we had a crystal ball in the past, but we could safely infer that certain patterns resulted in specific outcomes. It seems that is no longer true.

> The more volatile the world, the faster and more frequently things change – and the higher the element of surprise.

Complexity involves multiple factors at play, with greater variety and interconnection. In such an environment, it is hard to analyse and work out what to do. Imagine you are faced with a big bag of cables and wires, all jumbled up. You're pulling on one line, and you know other people are pulling on others, but you can't see inside the bag. That's what solving today's version of complexity looks like! You know the stakes are high, but you can't just hack into it with a knife. And if you don't communicate, you end up with a tight, impenetrable knot that is virtually impossible to unravel. Plenty of work problems can feel like that.

Ambiguity refers to a lack of clarity about how to interpret something. A situation is ambiguous, for example, when information is incomplete, contradicting or too inaccurate to draw clear conclusions. More generally it refers to fuzziness and vagueness in ideas and terminology. The more ambiguous the world, the harder it is to interpret. It's like being told you're looking at an orange, but being unsure if it's an actual orange, an orange ball or the sun – each of which requires a very different response.

Are these feeling familiar?

At least some of these characterise most work environments. The larger the organisation, the more likely you are to experience complexity and lack of clarity. In smaller organisations, you can often be caught out by volatility and ambiguity.

Chaos is not limited to organisations – most of us also have a particular style of chaos in which we function better than others. You might be able to pivot quickly from one plan to another or be comfortable with making decisions without all the information.

You could be really good at complex problem-solving, or someone who doesn't mind what outcome we land on.

In the following table, check the types of chaos you most frequently experience at work. Then mark those you least enjoy. Is there a correlation?

My work's chaos style	My least preferred style	My most preferred style
• Volatile • Unpredictable • Complex • Ambiguous	• Volatile • Unpredictable • Complex • Ambiguous	• Volatile • Unpredictable • Complex • Ambiguous

Figure 7: Chaos diagnostic

Below, I've outlined my top tactics for managing each style of chaos. Read them all or go straight to the ones that represent your work experience and that which you least prefer.

Assess all the tools that might be useful to you. There's no point being a mechanic with only one screwdriver – leaders today need a toolkit bristling with the right equipment to tackle any scenario.

Volatility

To handle sudden and unexpected changes, cultivate operational excellence.

If your workplace is characterised by unexpected and unstable changes of plan, and especially if you're not one for surprises, then you and I have something in common. I

> To handle sudden and unexpected changes, cultivate operational excellence.

don't do well with volatility, and I have had to work extra hard to cultivate the skills to cope in such situations.

My number one recommendation for navigating volatility is in your preparation – building a clear capacity for adaptation into all your plans.

What does that mean?

- Plan: All plans are subject to change, so expect the unexpected. As we discussed earlier, a pre-mortem planning session is absolutely gold for this. It's the second planning session you have, as the first assumes that everything will go right. The pre-mortem believes that everything will go wrong and decides what you'll do when that happens.

- Engage: Brief your team that plans and priorities may change and the reasons behind it. They can anticipate that you may ask them to do something different because the circumstances demand it and not because you are capricious. They also accept that sometimes you'll need to be directive because the circumstances require it, rather than because you're a tyrant.

- Result: Your team can mobilise and reshape quickly, and without delay, to where the work is. They are not hindered by micromanagement, performance penalties for changing priority, or by structures and budgets.

My sister is a competitive ocean sailor in her spare time. It sounds like hell to me, but we've already established that I don't like surprises, and that pretty much sums up ocean racing – especially around Australia!

Listening to her harrowing stories has long made me realise that leading in a volatile environment is like being a skipper. There's an overall course set, but that's not what the crew trains for. They train for the unexpected – rogue waves, sudden storms, and injury. The way a skipper handles it is to prepare his crew to know their job and need minimum supervision. They need to be prepared to move suddenly and without warning, and – when things get dicey – to take direction without debate.

Uncertainty

To decide in uncertainty, network for more information and then eliminate your options.

We are constantly developing new patterns about how work works, and any trust in the old ways that governed our decision-making is fast disappearing. It often feels like everything is a new challenge that no-one has ever faced before, or as though you are piecing together a complex and incomplete jigsaw.

> To decide in uncertainty, network for more information and then eliminate your options.

Your decision-making process is rich with what you don't know, and light on what you do know. So first we network for more information and then use a process of elimination to help land on the most likely answer.

Don't work, network

If you aren't sure you have the full picture, the best bet is to ask around. Try to identify who can provide the missing information. Who is closest to the missing puzzle piece or is a well-connected corporate gossip? These are useful people to know and could fill in enough gaps to give you confidence.

When faced with something new with an unpredictable outcome, the great news is that someone somewhere has probably met something similar – perhaps even quite recently – and they can fill important gaps for you. That's why peer networks and industry mentors are proving so popular. B-Suite leaders are retraining their brains to ask first, rather than try to work it out alone.

In these circumstances, your network is your most important asset, so if you are not a member of an industry tribe, association or community, join one now and get active asking questions, sharing wins and failures. The fastest way to learn about new patterns of cause and effect is by sharing our collective experiences.

Eliminate the available options to reach a decision

The brain focuses on existing evidence and prefers to ignore absent evidence. It doesn't do well with gaps, only with facts.

When faced with all the information, we can make decisions based on determination, or what something *will* be, such as $2 + 2 = 4$. But when there's little information, we have to base decisions on elimination, or what something *can't* be. If you were good at algebra, this would make sense to you, such as $2 + x = 4$. But of course, most work problems are not even algebra-simple, are they?

'It's elementary, my dear fellow.'

– Sherlock Holmes.

Sherlock Holmes was amazing at solving problems. As a detective, his skill was in using the gaps between the facts just as successfully as he used the facts themselves. He focused on the unknown as well as the known. Not being as brilliant as Holmes, I use a simple known/unknown model to help me work out the facts and gaps I have to work with, and what action I need to take to fill in those gaps and make a confident decision.

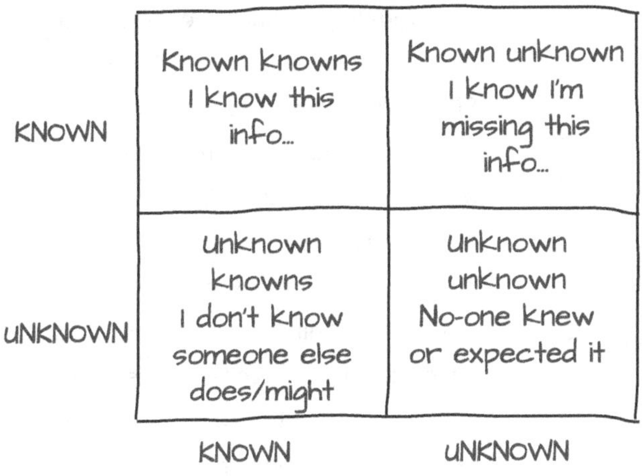

	KNOWN	UNKNOWN
KNOWN	Known knowns I know this info…	Known unknown I know I'm missing this info…
UNKNOWN	Unknown knowns I don't know someone else does/might	Unknown unknown No-one knew or expected it

Figure 8: A process of elimination

If you need to get better at this, try retraining your brain with logic puzzles, or get stuck into Cluedo. They will help you learn to make rapid and reliable decisions based on what you don't know, almost as readily as those based on what you do know.

Complexity

Dealing with multiple interconnected and moving parts means you need to bring in the experts. We're in a world now where the slightest tug on one strand can seriously mess up something elsewhere. And technology has only made this worse. The great thing about complexity is that it lends itself to subject matter experts. As leaders, our job is to bring those people together in a room with a clear set of objectives, then leave them to get on with it.

> As leaders, our job is to bring those people together in a room with a clear set of objectives, then leave them to get on with it.

Your challenge is to frame the challenge appropriately and ensure a shared understanding and translation between these SMEs. You may need to arbitrate between conflicting opinions from time to time but otherwise get out of their way – unless you are a deep expert and can afford to be locked in that room until the deadline. Complexity is not something you can dip in and out of successfully. It needs focus, patience and meticulous attention to detail, so make sure the people you put on the task have the expertise, the attitude and uninterrupted space to solve the problem.

Ambiguity

Almost single-handedly responsible for the popularity of Agile, ambiguity is that uncomfortable state of not being able to see things clearly – the problem, the pathway to solving it, or the endpoint. I always think of agile problem-solvers as explorers.

They're not quite sure what is around the next corner and what that will require of them, so they explore, test, learn and iterate as they go.

The iterative nature of Agile lends itself to ambiguous scenarios where nothing is clear. In order to manage your risks and get the best quality outcome, you can only work it out through a process of experimentation. The most common steps of Agile experimentation are closely aligned to the classic scientific experimentation methods:

- Purpose: Make sure your objectives are clear and concise; otherwise you'll wander into 'interesting but not relevant' territory pretty quickly!

- Observation: Spend your time making sure you've got the right problem statement – that you are not inferring what you see, but focusing on the facts. The right problem statement will make or break your experiment.

- Hypothesis: Agree your theory and the assumptions that underpin it.

- Experiment: Test it, see if it works as anticipated.

- Analysis: Assess the results. What didn't work as expected, and how might you resolve that? What did work and can be leveraged?

Knowing how to respond to varying types of chaos helps your situational leadership and your decision-making capabilities. It means you can make an accurate call on the right response and mobilise the right resources to tackle any scenario with success.

Use the Space

'Your ability to solve problems and
make good decisions is the true
measure of your skill as a leader.'

– Brian Tracy

Now that we've learned to control the pace of work by coping, prioritising, planning and deciding in a more structured and communicable way (including plenty of delegation and deprioritisation, I hope!) – you have more space to think.

B-Suite leaders have rarely been taught to slow down or to think strategically. Instead, they are bred for action, to lead execution. In most traditional organisations, strategic thinking has been the domain of the C-Suite.

> B-Suite leaders have rarely been taught to slow down or to think strategically.

The problem with this top-down approach means that the C-Suite is presumed to develop the vision, set the goals and priorities, make the big decisions and drive performance.

Yet as business becomes faster and more disruptive, it's the B-Suite that takes up these responsibilities to drive the business forward.

As we've discussed, the role of the B-Suite leader today is to ensure their teams cope, prioritise, plan and decide direction multiple times in a single day. Sometimes this aligns with the corporate or functional strategy, but most often it does not.

If this was left to the C-Suite, the business couldn't keep up with the pace. Relying on top-down communication, decision-making and prioritisation would create bottlenecks, inaction and frustration – and the business would lose.

Performance is almost exclusively the domain of the B-Suite because they are responsible for the motivation, engagement, and discretionary effort of their teams. The C-Suite is too far removed to make much impact on discretionary effort, but the B-Suite's mark is indelible.

The B-Suite need to solve more problems and make more decisions than the C-Suite, so enhancing the B-Suite's ability to think strategically and problem-solve complexity is becoming increasingly valuable and urgent.

Most B-Suiters I know complain about not having the time to think. But here's what is really going on.

They've not been trained to slow down, so they think too fast and pressure themselves into taking action – as this is where they feel their value (and comfort) lies.

When they do think, it's often only at surface level. This is great for quick-fix problem-solving but can mean treating the symptom rather than the cause, creating rework and problems that are never resolved.

Many B-Suiters don't have confidence in their thinking processes, so they second guess themselves and lack the courage of their convictions.

Using the space well is central to your ability to start operating like the C-Suite.

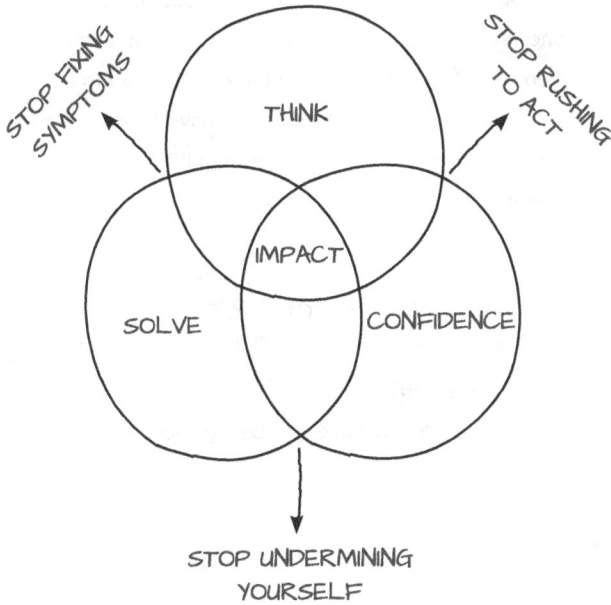

Figure 9: Use the space

This section covers three ways to do so:

1. Think

2. Solve

3. Have Confidence

Think

Slow down, and think things through, even when you are under pressure to decide quickly.

One of my C-Suite mentors ran a huge business worth billions of dollars and had a fearsome reputation as both a strategic thinker and operational genius. I once asked her about the most important lesson she learned transitioning from the B-Suite to the C-Suite. She replied: 'The very moment that you feel you have to act quickly is almost inevitably the moment that you have to slow down, and think things through. And once you are confident enough to hold your nerve, the shift has occurred.'

We've been trained to prize busy above all else, haven't we? If anyone asks about your week, isn't the answer almost always 'busy'? And we say that proudly, right? As in — look how much stamina I have, how productive I'm being, how this is a sign that business is good. Right?

Wrong.

Surely busy is actually a *bad* thing? Isn't it an indicator that we are working harder, not smarter? What if the next time you were asked, you answered 'thoughtful', 'productive' or 'impactful' instead of 'busy'?

Our brain is like a two-speed bicycle; with one gear for cruising and one for pushing uphill. The cruising gear is what Daniel Kahneman calls System One Thinking; it is automatic, instinctive, and effortless (Kahneman, 2011). This kind of thinking can become so honed that your gut feeling can overrule all other evidence and you'll still go with it – you instinctively know what to do (Gladwell, 2005).

Many B-Suite leaders operate in this gear most of the time – it helps them race through a million tasks, decisions, and actions largely without having to think consciously. As we are typically quite expert here, things just happen in the flow of being busy.

And there is the trap. It feels easy, so we fall into it without noticing. It's the comfort blanket of thinking for most B-Suite leaders: it's one of our coping mechanisms.

It's the second gear that most of us have to learn to engage and keep engaged. What Kahneman calls 'slow thinking' is far more complex and mentally draining. It's the kind of thinking when you can almost feel the wheels creaking in your head and makes you rub your forehead. Slow thinking is what you have to exert when adjusting your behaviour for a board meeting or presenting at a huge conference.

These moments feel intense because we are typically not as skilled in slow thinking, and that's why slowing things down and starting to think deeply can be such a challenge to so many B-Suite leaders. We are so used to operating in System One, that we don't know how to switch on System Two when we have the space to do so.

My number one tactic for learning to slow down and think things through is to adopt the habit of positive procrastination.

Many of us are masters at negative procrastination (not getting things done), and some have perfected the art of pre-crastination (getting them done ahead of schedule). Still, few of us have the confidence to hold off until the last minute in favour of a better outcome.

It sounds risky, doesn't it? Because it goes against what we've been taught – to think on your feet and get busy. But it's not, so let me explain.

First: Think about how you are going to think

Metacognition refers to thinking about thinking and how to manage all the variables involved. This is like making a plan about *how* to think before we allow ourselves to think:

- Person variables: What we recognise about our strengths and weaknesses in learning and processing information, e.g. 'I don't like doing budgets so...'
- Task variables: What we know or can figure out about the nature of a task and the processing demands required to complete it. 'I know this will take me longer, and I can't get distracted.'
- Strategy variables: The strategies we can use to solve the problem, e.g. research, network, delegate. 'I'll talk with my finance business partner to make sure I understand it fully before I start.'

Once you've got the plan clear and you've done your pre-work (like talking to your finance business partner), then you can allow yourself to think.

If we don't do the pre-work, we often find ourselves thinking about things from the wrong angle – it's a waste of mental energy, and that's why procrastination is such a useful tool!

Second: Ask a *lot* of questions

Most of us are taught to fear and loathe procrastination. We are proud of being action-oriented and solution-focused, and any form of 'dragging your heels' is regarded as a type of failure.

I used to sneer at those with a 'procrastination problem', but then I started to understand, admire and now use procrastination with my coaching clients and in my own life.

A few years ago, I learned an important lesson that made me decide busy was bad, and procrastination could be positive.

I was working on a new digital product with a scrum master who made me wait what felt like months before he let the team start building anything.

And just when I thought I couldn't take it any longer, and my action-oriented inner voice was at screaming pitch, he made me wait another week, so they could ask more questions.

Further delays when my nerves were frayed, and with a looming deadline made that one of the hardest weeks of my career. I couldn't stand what I thought was inactivity. There was some online gaming happening, and discussions over coffee. There were plenty of walking breaks, but no Developing going on!

But the waiting worked. The minute they picked up tools, the team produced a brilliant quality product at lightning speed with hardly any rework or wastage.

This taught me the importance of waiting, framing the question properly, reviewing all the angles and then putting it off just a little bit longer to see if your brain spots something else before you make a start.

Third: Sleep on it

> *'If it weren't for the last minute,*
> *nothing would get done.'*
>
> – Rita Mae Brown

Whenever faced with a difficult decision, a complex proposal or designing a complicated workshop, I insist on sleeping on it before I start to design. I suspect I come over to my clients as a little eccentric with my insistence on this, but it's a critical part of my thought process, and ultimately, it delivers them a great result.

It turns out this isn't eccentric; it's scientific. In his book, *Wait: The Art and Science of Delay*, Frank Partnoy writes that when faced with a decision, we should assess how long we have to make it, and then wait until the last possible moment to do so (Partnoy, 2012).

> Whenever faced with a difficult decision, a complex proposal or designing a complicated workshop, I insist on sleeping on it before I start to design.

The argument (which I fully support) is that delaying decisions enables you to make sounder decisions.

When faced with difficult, complex, or important decisions, he advises you to ask yourself this one question. 'What is the maximum amount of time I have available to respond?'

This is a great frame to develop the habit of slow thinking. For example, instead of starting to write a business case on day -30, you resist writing it until day -3, and spend the other 27 days framing, asking questions and thinking things through. The act of writing is fast thinking, and should be done last.

By reversing our normal tendency – which is to get busy, quick – we are also learning to manage our pre-crastination and perfectionist tendencies.

Pre-crastinators are those who submit their items weeks ahead of deadline. This reflects a misguided sense of productivity that values activity over quality. If you think you've got this habit, be careful, it's a classic underminer for many B-Suite leaders and dangerous to cultivate if you want to level up your impact.

Perfectionists will spend those 27 days perfecting their business case, instead of using the time to think things through. Adopting a positive procrastination frame of mind can ensure we apply the maximum time to think it through, and the minimum time to worry about perfecting it.

In his TED talk, psychologist Adam Grant describes an experiment in which individuals were tasked with coming up with business ideas. They could either start brainstorming right away or play Minesweeper for a few minutes before getting started. It turns out the Minesweepers were 16 per cent more creative than the others (Grant, 2016).

'Sleeping on it' is there for a reason. It enables you to access some of that bonus brainpower and means that when you finally sit down to design, decide or problem-solve, you'll do easier, faster and better quality work.

Solve

'If I had one hour to save the world, I would spend fifty-five minutes defining the problem and only five minutes finding the solution.'

— Albert Einstein

> Problem-solving is one of those 'future skills' that we needed yesterday, and one of those 'soft skills' that are really hard.

Problem-solving is one of those 'future skills' that we needed yesterday, and one of those 'soft skills' that are really hard. We know that pace and complexity is accelerating, so our ability to solve increasingly complex problems – quickly and accurately – is accelerating too.

The problem with problems today is that there are so many, they are so interdependent, and they are so complex. It makes your head hurt to just think about problems in general, let alone any one in particular.

All too often, I observe clients solving a problem only to create three more because of the interdependent nature of the one they tackled. Or I see one of many band-aids put on a leaking dam and wonder when they will realise they now have a legacy of band-aids to unravel and underneath there's still a leaking dam. This is rework we cannot afford as we continue to do more with less.

So how can we tackle problem-solving in a different way?

First, frame your problem

'A problem well stated is a problem half solved.'

– John Dewey

Too often we jump into problem-solving without fully understanding the problem first. We think we know what it is, and we move into solution mode. Perhaps we've seen something like this before, and we know what worked.

Trained to take action, this often leads many B-Suite managers to get busy without having a clear understanding of the end goal. And without being certain they've even selected the right problem to work on.

Get clear on your goal. What exactly is going to change as a result of you doing this. This will help you to stay on target with your 'fixing'. There are plenty of DIY dads who were asked to fix a leak in the roof and ended up putting on an entire extension. That's especially awkward if, in their DIY dad enthusiasm, they failed to fix the leak or caused an even bigger problem.

Get clear on your priorities. Are you fixing problems in the high-value section of your strategic prioritisation matrix, or are you getting distracted or pressured into fixing problems in the low-value section? Are you fixing the problems in a logical sequence, or are you fixing the noisiest one first?

Consult on the problem. Use your network to consult broadly on the issue as you see it – you will undoubtedly find that you're missing a particular perspective from your original view. Spend time engaging and aligning all potential stakeholders in defining the problem before you get to work on it.

Resist solving the problem – yet. People are far more open to new information, considerations and implications when they are in *thinking* mode. Once they move into *doing* mode, that same new information, consideration or implication usually means delays, derailment or sunk costs, and we become resistant rather than open.

Any changes, however slight, to the problem statement at this stage, will result in different solutions later on, so it's really important to spend time here. An oversight at this stage could mean that while you solve the problem for one area, you create another elsewhere.

Then, clarify assumptions

Be very specific with your understanding. Don't let anyone make assumptions as these will derail you from the outset.

Challenge anything that's an exaggeration or generalisation; they are simply not helpful.

Define anything with an ambiguous meaning. For example, 'leadership' or 'strategy' are both classic words that everyone thinks they understand, yet can't agree on a definition. Make sure these aren't floating around to undermine you when it's too late.

Define subjective standards. 'Too expensive' or 'not enough' are not helpful phrases when you are trying to be precise. Define the right price and the right level before you move ahead or inevitably you'll miss the mark when the solution lands because the mark was never clarified in the first place.

> Kerry was about to go ahead with investing in the resources necessary to fix a problem in onboarding new clients. She had one final call to make to frame the issue – with her finance leader. And thank goodness she did! Had Kerry gone ahead and implemented the solution she had in mind, she'd have broken a really important quality assurance mechanism put in place by the finance team to avoid overpayment of commissions. These had previously cost millions and had disastrous impacts on morale. Instead, Kerry was able identify a win/win option that delivered a better client experience, less effort from her team, and protected the finance mechanism even better than before. And instead of making a fairly public mistake, she carved a name for herself as a great collaborator.

Finally, avoid fixing the wrong problem

'We fail more often because we solve the wrong problem than because we get the wrong solution to the right problem.'
– Russell L. Ackoff

There are so many problems in our workplaces that sometimes it's hard to know which to pick up and run with, and which to leave well alone. But if we don't choose the right ones, we may end up with a reputation as someone who tinkers with everything and makes no significant impact on anything.

Once you've spent some time framing your problem, you'll probably find you have uncovered multiple root causes. You might even feel further away from the problem being solved rather than closer to it. That is where this next exercise comes in handy.

List out your potential problem statements. That's all the root causes. There will be plenty of these, as there is never just one when you are dealing with any level of complexity.

And most of them will be the wrong problem to solve.

Big, complex organisations are FULL of problems, you literally trip over them and work around them every day. Yet we often pick the wrong ones to tackle.

Here are the four most common offenders:

1. Distractions: problems that are not directly related to your goal. These are likely to be highly solvable (that's part of their appeal), but they are merely distractions.

    They may be a problem, even a really big one, but unless they directly relate to your goal, they are not your problem. At least not right now, as they add no value.

    One of my coaching clients had a penchant for solving distractions. It meant he was incredibly busy, and lots of people were grateful to him for fixing up the small stuff, but he failed to drive a reputation as a complex problem-solver. The irony was that he was exceptional at problem-solving. His weakness was choosing the right problem to solve.

2. Good from afar, but far from good: problems that look right, but are not.

We, humans, love to make assumptions, don't we? So much so that Daniel Kahneman calls our brain 'a machine for leaping to conclusions'. It's absolutely determined to land an answer to every problem. And therein lies our challenge as leaders seeking to solve complex problems.

I frequently see leaders tackling problems that look good from a distance, but in reality, are the opposite. They seem relevant but aren't, or appear to have a high impact on your goal but don't.

> Our desire to leap to conclusions means we frequently make assumptions on face value.

Our desire to leap to conclusions means we frequently make assumptions on face value. This can mean projects are cancelled because we can't immediately see causation, or we press on with projects where the causation is assumed.

It shows up most often when a leader inherits a portfolio and makes decisions to progress or cancel initiatives that prove to be wrong. We need to evaluate every project to determine if we are working on the right problem.

3. Immovable Objects: Problems that are bigger than your goal

One problem I often see leaders stubbornly trying to tackle is the 'immovable object'.

These are problems that affect your goal but are really wicked – difficult, big and curly. The chances are they impact far more than just you and your goal. The most common are structural, legislative, industrial, or technological, for example, 'Our Industrial Award prevents us from doing XYZ with our workforce' or 'If we had better technology, we could....'.

It's not that they can't be solved, but in the context of your goal, addressing that problem is likely to overstretch your project.

- Is your goal big enough to warrant the effort?
- Are your timeframes long enough to see it through?
- Will your budget stretch to trying to solve that on your way to achieving your goal?
- Is this a smart use of your investment?

Choose to simply work-around the immovable object and leave that particular battle for another day. Be the river, not the rock.

4. The Duplicate: A problem someone else is already working on.

The issue with problem-solving is not actually in finding the solution; it's in defining the problem. In fact, the process of defining often presents a solution, yet, oddly, not at all when tackled the other way around.

Often one of the fastest and easiest ways to solve your problem is to share it. The chances are that if you've spotted it, so will someone else – and that person may already be working on it.

Perhaps surprisingly, I find many leaders resist the perceived effort it takes to engage broadly and consult widely before a project kicks off. They tell me it takes too long, throws up too many barriers, and in the end, they can't get anything done.

Yet duplicated effort is one of the most frustrating things a leader can experience, especially since we are all doing so much more with so much less.

By sharing your problem, you may uncover work already being done on it or something similar. Your opportunity is to share your goal broadly in the hope of including their efforts and accelerating your outcome, or you can re-focus their perspective to support a win-win.

> By sharing your problem, you may uncover work already being done on it or something similar.

With this approach, you'll not only make sure you have defined and aligned on the goal state but that you have evaluated and prioritised what problem(s) to solve to get it 'fixed'. You've avoided miscommunication and misaligned expectations, and you've been as robust as possible with avoiding rework and mistakes.

Once all this preparatory problem-solving work is done, you may find the solution is far easier to achieve than you realised. You've likely half-solved it already, so when you finally get into building your solution, you're moving quickly and with confidence.

Confidence

> *'Trying to teach leadership without first*
> *building confidence is like building a*
> *house on a foundation of sand.'*
>
> – Francisco Dao

Confidence is another holy grail of leadership. We all want it, and we think everyone else has it.

A lack of confidence in how you're using the space to think and problem-solve can undermine you and your leadership impact. Many B-Suite leaders have a complex relationship with confidence, and it results in them second-guessing themselves, lacking the courage of their convictions, or failing to take actions that would significantly benefit their careers.

Few B-Suite leaders share this openly, but I suppose that's the value of having a trusted mentor to share with. Every B-Suite leader (or C-Suite leader, now I come to think of it) I've ever coached has issues with their confidence. Some from time to time, and others all the time.

Confidence is a key enabler of the ability to hold the Space to think. Without it, we easily tumble back into being busy, which is the place where we are expert, where our progress (or at least activity) is measurable, and where we feel most confident. When asked, most B-Suite leaders say they feel most confident in the Pace and least confident in the Space.

It is logical to find it harder to derive value from strategic thinking than from taking action. One is tangible, while the other is not. Yet in truth, that's not our logic talking; it's our confidence.

When confidence fails us – when we undermine our own opinions or second guess our decisions, we sabotage our impact. We simply won't go for impact in the same way, which is why it is so important to work on this every day.

So how do we hold both our nerve and the Space, when there are so many conflicting priorities, looming deadlines and B-Suite busyness is threatening to crush us?

Confidence is a sly fox – the unpredictable critter can turn around and bite us at the most inopportune moments. So let's take it to puppy school!

> Confidence is a sly fox – the unpredictable critter can turn around and bite us at the most inopportune moments.

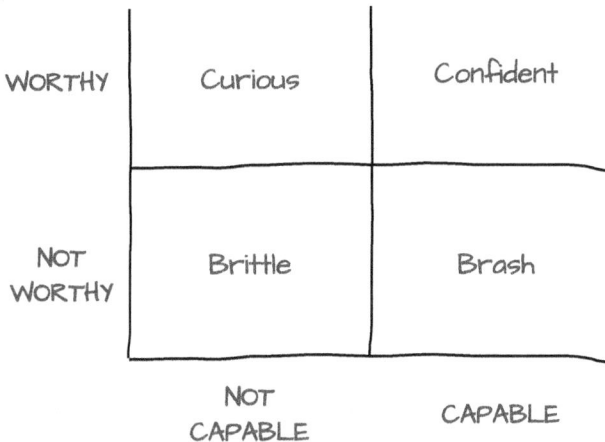

Figure 10: Confidence

Phases of confidence

Confidence is made up of two key factors:

- Our sense of worthiness: 'I'm not good enough *for* it'.

  This is where we doubt our right to be at the table, compare ourselves to others, and listen to our inner voice a little too often. Sometimes deep-rooted in self-esteem and at others just being thrown off your stride, our sense of self-worth is the most precarious of the two confidence drivers and the harder to control.

- Our sense of capability: 'I'm not good enough *at* it'.

  Given we humans are our own worst critics, most B-Suite leaders have a strong awareness of their gaps. In a few seconds, they can readily rattle off a list of gaps, weaknesses or development areas, while struggling to find positives in twice the amount of time. So it's natural to start from a place of 'lack' (I don't have enough) rather than one of 'abundance' (I've got more than enough). The good news is this is an entirely learnable driver of confidence, so we can form the habit of saying 'I'm not good enough at it – yet'.

  Capability-related confidence is fixable. Training, practise, mentoring and peer networking all help to build the belief that we can do it or that we will soon be able to. If you're feeling you don't know enough about a subject to be confident, or you're facing a problem you've never dealt with before, or a career opportunity that daunts you, ask for help to develop your capabilities and bridge that gap.

The interplay between our sense of capability and sense of worth can result in a visible change to our confidence levels. This affects performance and presentation; both of which are essential for leadership success.

Because confidence is so unpredictable, it's essential to have some ready tactics to get it moving in the right direction.

Look again at Figure 10 and let's walk through the four stages with practical strategies to level up your confidence.

Confident. This is the goal – it's where your capability meets your worthiness. Here you balance both your right to be at the table and your contribution to the conversation. In the B-Suite, we are faced every day with situations that challenge our confidence levels. We walk into a room with more senior people and suddenly feel not so capable. Or we listen to an inspirational speaker and walk away feeling somehow less worthy. A new member joins the committee, which changes the dynamic and impacts your sense of self-worth. Or perhaps they deliver new information that undermines what you thought to be true and impacts your confidence in your capability.

But every time your confidence goes off track, there are tactics you can deploy to bring you back.

Curious. These people are usually the ones asking loads of questions, with an inner confidence that means none of those questions feels stupid. They feel worthy but are not convinced of their capability. They recognise that if you know that you don't know, then ask.

Frame your questions in ways that boost your confidence. 'Pretend I know nothing about this project, and brief me in will you?' 'I do know about it, but I'd like your version.' Or, 'I'm not across the detail yet, what do I need to know?' And don't forget to ask for reading material – familiarity with the latest paper or communication deck on the topic will quickly build your knowledge and capability so you can move into Confidence.

> Melissa was asked to step across to run a project that was in trouble. Well-known for her ability to turn things around in her field of expertise, this was the first time she was venturing into a brand new field. The project was high profile, was failing, and she didn't know the first thing about the content. She was terrified. To mask her terror, she played the 'pretend I know nothing' game with enough gravitas that everyone thought she knew something – and eventually, she did.

Brash. Most of us have observed this behaviour in others, but may not be as objective about observing it in ourselves. Remember that colleague that was a bit show-offy? Who kept reminding us that they've done this before at their previous employer and that they are the expert? This behaviour is typically the result of a conflict in confidence drivers – high competence and low worthiness.

This is the deception of confidence – it hides a low sense of worth under a veneer of knowing it all.

If you're feeling a little intimidated by a situation or person, then beware of using your credentials to state your value. To present as 'worthy', even if you're feeling 'unworthy', simply remind yourself to ask instead of tell. This will dispel the brashness and remind you that you do measure up and you are worthy.

> Karl was feeling a bit overwhelmed as the newest leader in the team. The rest of the leadership team had worked together for more than three years, were known for being high performers, and were individually impressive. Karl had gone through an extensive interview process to get this role, and knew that it indicated he was the top ten per cent in the market, but he was still feeling pretty intimidated. His reaction was to make a good first impression, so to cover his nerves, he reassured everyone they had made a good decision by asserting his credentials every chance he had. Karl's manager took him aside and told him to chill out: he had already passed the test, but his reputation and relationships were being coloured by showing off.

Brittle. When feeling neither worthy nor capable, we can become brittle in our delivery. This is often B-Suite leaders at their least impactful. Their confidence is visibly shaken, their coping mechanisms are low, and whatever triggered this crisis will be spilling into all other aspects of their job, affecting their ability to control the pace, use the space or make the case. It will hit their productivity, strategic thinking and influence all at once if they are not careful. To manage a brittle moment, try to take a step back and lean on your coping mechanisms. If all you're up to today is doing the washing up, then own that. Avoid unnecessary visibility, and ask for help. With your team, this could be your trusted direct reports who can hold the fort while you get your confidence back in hand. With your peers, a trusted ally can keep an eye on your public demeanour and minimise any personal brand damage. With your mentor, make an urgent phone call to get back on track.

Even if the last thing you feel like is reaching out when you're brittle, this is the absolutely the first thing to do. The longer you leave it, the more brittle you'll become.

Joy moved across the country into a senior role that was an absolute win for her career – more money, more authority, more visibility. Yet within weeks, the adrenaline had worn off, and she was feeling alone, vulnerable and incapable. She wasn't sure how to balance her approach with the team and was sinking into a vicious cycle where her low capability (which we had known) was beginning to impact her self-worth. She started to feel and behave in a brittle, fragile manner and was sinking into an 'I am not worthy, I am not capable' narrative.

Once we reasserted her reasons for being hired into the role, rather than focusing on her capability gaps, she was able to pull herself into curious mode, which helped her quickly learn what she lacked and put her back into confidence again.

Regularly check if you're out of balance

Your first job in actively managing your confidence is to identify where the balance has shifted. Is it a looming capability gap that has put you off balance, or is your sense of self-worth lower than usual today?

How do you identify that you're starting to get out of balance?

- You might feel under the weather: Your immune system is linked to resilience levels which impacts confidence. If you're under the weather, the chance of it affecting your confidence is high.

- Not sleeping well: Difficulty with sleeping is extremely common. It affects coping mechanisms which in turn influences your sense of self-worth. Do you see changes to your usual sleep pattern?

- Mood swings: Onset burnout or impacted resilience can unbalance our hormonal state, and this affects men and women equally. Are you experiencing any unusual emotional highs and lows? Snapping at those around you or crying more easily?

- Loss of control: When our sense of self-worth is low, we may find ourselves taking unusual risks. Over-drinking, spending too much, or taking reckless risks in relationships.

- Abnormal stress: Are you over-reacting to everyday irritants? Are things such as bad manners, poor driving, or bad service, making you unusually cross or nervous?

- Feeling paranoid about a colleague: Are you sensing that you're over-reacting to them or sensing a threat?

If any of these resonate, then adopt tactics that offer the best chance of recovering your equilibrium.

Nine self-worth refuellers

1. Tackle your inner voice, don't ignore it

Listen to it objectively and make a physical note of what is being said. Be specific. Write it down. Evaluate it. If there is any merit, decide on a course of action. If there isn't merit, actively move on from dwelling on non-specific self-negatives.

Liz's inner voice is called Desdemona. Desdemona is a very cruel, attractive and clever brunette who looks suspiciously like Nigella Lawson. When she starts to dominate the inner conversation, Liz reminds herself that she wouldn't choose Desdemona as a friend, so listening to her is illogical. Liz calls a real friend (or her mentor!) instead.

2. Learn to be an optimist

Your brain is wired for negativity 'like Velcro for negative experiences and Teflon for positive ones' (Hanson, n.d.). Rewire it by noticing your negativity, and search for a silver lining in the situation – even if it's unintended, good things often come out of even the most difficult situations. How might you finish this sentence 'The one good thing about all this is....'

3. Don't go a day without laughing

Laughter can temporarily block negative emotions, help you relax and recharge, and unite people during difficult times. Try these tips to increase your laughter quota. Get closer to those who are laughing (it's contagious!), laugh at yourself, laugh at situations rather than bemoan them, and strive to recall, read and share funny stories that happen rather than negative ones.

4. Offer your help

Helping others triggers the same centres in the brain as food and sex. It makes us feel good.

'Help' can be whatever you want it to be; I recommend something you enjoy doing, so it's never a chore.

Offer it proactively; being asked to help doesn't work on the endorphins in the same way. Ask for and accept help. Many people have a mental block about this, seeing it as a failure, weakness or sign of surrender.

Accepting help reinforces that it's okay to not be in control, you're not alone, and another perspective might be all you need. Try it.

5. Develop a growth mindset

Even though playing to your strengths reinforces your self-esteem, don't hide from your weaknesses, instead, seek to develop yourself in areas that matter to you.

6. Take regular breaks

Overwork and exhaustion are the enemies of self-esteem. We get tired and emotional all too easily.

> Overwork and exhaustion are the enemies of self-esteem.

Breaks should include a range of things such as daydreaming for a few minutes, leaving your desk every 90 minutes, clearing the weekend of work and taking at least 10 days a year as holiday.

7. Mindfulness

Some people are put off by prayer, meditation or yoga, but did you know mindfulness also includes doodling, puzzles or doing the dishes? These are all stress-busters that work because you are focusing hard on nothing, and that acts as a circuit breaker.

8. Food and exercise

Being active boosts your feel-good endorphins and distracts you from daily worries, building your self-esteem. Eating well is the core to physical wellbeing. Start small; but just start.

9. Sleep

A lack of sleep is a famously effective form of torture. Try to be disciplined around your sleep patterns, with regular sleep and wake times. Avoid late-night alcohol, caffeine, meals, electronic blue light and exercise. Set your room to cool or try a warm bath to drop your body temperature.

Six capability refuellers

1. Play to your strengths most of the time

We tend to enjoy the activities that we are better at, and in turn, get better at the activities we enjoy. Be clear on what you are good at and learn to value it. Others already do (just ask them), and this will reinforce your confidence levels. Where you don't feel strong, take confidence from your progress. Every black belt was once a white belt. If you're feeling not good at something, just add a *yet* to the end of it......

2. Lean in

Make connections: Many valuable relationships, pieces of advice, humour and learning have come from a casual chat.

Seek advice: We can't all be experts in all things. Nor does anyone have the time to track down every interesting idea. When you spend time connecting with others, you have the opportunity to gain from their knowledge and share your own.

Share your experience: Working and pursuing your career can be lonely. One of the best benefits of taking the time to connect with other professionals is that they understand your journey. When you are facing challenges or frustrations, a trusted friend can prove invaluable. The best time to find a true friend is before you need one.

3. Have purpose

Take a long-term view: remembering to look at your long-term goals will put current state setbacks and gaps into perspective.

But set short-term goals: keeping goals short (no more than 30 days) means that the goals are more relatable and achievable. That leads to action, which in turn reinforces your sense of achievement and capability.

4. Clarify the 'what'

Being specific on what outcomes are sought is critical to being purposeful. What are we looking to achieve in this meeting? What do I want from this relationship? If you know what you are aiming for, you'll find yourself feeling more capable of achieving it.

5. Take action

Stop your planning brain from getting excited about lots of options and start narrowing them down to just pick one. Otherwise, you'll never take action.

6. Expect the unexpected

These days, all plans are subject to change. If we expect this, we reduce our anxiety when it happens, and we enhance our resourcefulness by re-planning. Traffic jam? No problem, just find another route.

Having the confidence to hold the space so that you can solve the right problems and think things through thoroughly means that you are capable of being strategic all day long. It takes practise, but it's a life skill that's worth paying attention to.

This increases your team's ability to be innovative and impactful and makes you (and your function) more productive and valuable to your organisation. It makes you more transferrable as a leader and starts to really elevate your style from the B-Suite, where the *work* traditionally gets done, to the C-Suite – where the *thinking* traditionally gets done.

Make the Case

'The key to successful leadership
today is influence, not authority.'
– Ken Blanchard

Choose influence for impact

A lack of influence is a significant leadership complaint, yet many leaders regard deliberate attempts to determine outcomes as undesirable.

In his book, *To Sell is Human*, Daniel Pink estimated that 40 per cent of a leader's day involves influencing – persuading, directing and pitching – but I think the percentage is much higher (Pink, 2012).

The amount of time we dedicate to making a case is the notable difference between a hard-working leader and a high-impact leader. It's the last section of this book for a reason. By controlling the pace and using the space to be strategic, your influencing efforts will be more targeted, easier and more successful.

While influence matters to every leadership mode, it's particularly important for Innovators, who are looking to make the difficult transition from leading *how* the works gets done, to influencing *what* work gets done.

An influential leader is an expert at identifying which conversations need to happen to remove roadblocks, seize opportunities, or slow things down. It's another big lever to use when making the shift from working in your business to working on your business. Your ability to influence in all directions is crucial for your teams to succeed.

Impact requires a commitment of time, thought and effort to influence in all directions – even if you don't like the sound of deliberate influence. As you become a high-impact leader, your to-do list will include growing proportions of influencing activity – but starting this new habit can often be difficult.

> To *have* influence, we have to be prepared to *exert* influence.

Many of my clients roll their eyes at the concept of deliberate influence and consider it to be political, manipulative or Machiavellian. They want their work to speak for itself. But work can't speak. You have to do it – or you are leaving your hard work to chance.

To *have* influence, we have to be prepared to *exert* influence.

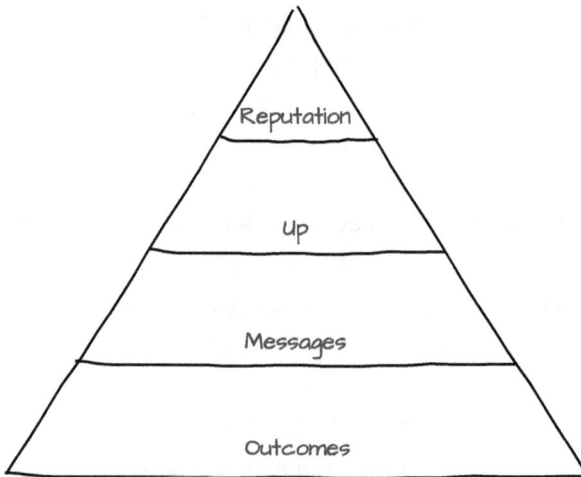

Figure 11: Make the case

There are four areas in which you need to be conscious of exerting influence and deliberately making a case with every interaction.

Daniel Pink says that leadership is sales. Most leaders cringe when they hear this. I do too. Why? Because our baked-in impression of sales is icky – we don't want to be seen as deliberately manipulating situations to go our way.

Let me ask – have you ever had one of these thoughts?

- 'My work should speak for itself.'
- 'I'm the expert; you should take my word for it.'
- 'I see I'm going to have to persuade you.'
- 'How do I get you to help me achieve my goal?'
- 'How do you make them think it's their idea?'

Maybe you've had several, or perhaps all of them. I certainly have.

The concept of developing influencing skills has historically been driven by the sales industry, with experts such as Robert Cialdini and Mike Weinberg leading the charge.

And that's why we're all so familiar with older-style influencing techniques, such as:

- Show – like a door-to-door vacuum cleaner salesman or product demonstrator
- Tell – the assertion that you should get something because it is cutting-edge
- Diagnose – asking enough questions to ensure your product meets at least some of your stakeholders' needs.

> A contemporary approach requires a more brain-based view, where we think about what others need, rather than what we want.

A contemporary approach requires a more brain-based view, where we think about what others need, rather than what we want. And in particular when we are:

Managing outcomes. As we start to operate outside the remit of our functions, managing outcomes becomes recognisably more important and more difficult. We are doing it through influence and partnership with others, rather than through direct authority over our teams alone. This is where the majority of your influencing effort and time should sit.

Managing messaging. You continually communicate with your team, but how often do you think about the case you are presenting with every email or call? It can feel like more work to commit to using language as a powerful tool, when, in fact, it creates less. This is the second most common space in which to apply your influence.

Managing up. You need a great working relationship with your leader – it's the most important one you have. A great leader will lift your game, while a bad one will make you want to quit. If the relationship isn't working, then it's at least 50 per cent your fault. (Yes, it is!) Your team suffers, and so do you, so invest heavily in making this work.

Managing your reputation. Whether you like it or not, you already have a reputation or a brand. It's what people say about you when you're not in the room. Most leaders loathe the thought of managing their personal brand – until they get to a certain level and then they wish they'd done it sooner. It's the least time-consuming of the activities under Making the Case, and one that most B-Suite leaders neglect. Your reputation is a powerful tool for impact, so hone it and use it well.

Let's look at each of these in-depth.

Managing outcomes

'No one saves us but ourselves. No one can, and no one may. We ourselves must walk the path.'

– Buddha

As we learn – or aspire – to have more impact, and to work on our business rather than in it, a growing proportion of each day should be spent on managing outcomes. This means engaging in successful collaboration and negotiation on behalf of your team. The impact of doing this well is that your team can continue to move at pace, and without disruption. Typically, as the key decision-maker, it's you who holds those conversations and make those decisions. (And if that's not yet you, then see the next section on Managing Up and bring your leader to the right conversations.)

As businesses become increasingly complex, and the nature of work more integrated, we need to be better at collaboration and negotiation.

> As businesses become increasingly complex, and the nature of work more integrated, we need to be better at collaboration and negotiation.

Kirsten was struggling to collaborate with her peer; Illona. Her view was that Illona was deliberately undermining the negotiation by refusing to compromise, and was dead against the whole concept. But upon investigation, it turned out that Illona was very keen on the idea, as long as her team didn't absorb more administrative work. She was so much in favour that she was willing to tip in some additional funding – especially if there was an opportunity to reduce the admin burden not just avoid it.

As Kirsten hadn't understood this before she started, the first item she wanted across the line had backfired. She had proposed a solution that created more admin for Illona's team. Because Illona disagreed, Kirsten assumed poor intent and even accused Illona of undermining the goal. Understandably, Illona was offended and became defensive and sceptical of the negotiation process and Kirsten's approach. In her mind, Kirsten was playing to win, so Illona conservatively scrutinised every item before giving an inch. And that extra budget? Off the table.

Stay-in not buy-in

Many of my client organisations have invested heavily in the formal infrastructure that supports greater collaboration: Agile ways of working, collaboration training, open-plan offices, restructures. But in many cases, it isn't going exactly to plan. I hear complaints that their efforts are not sticking, and are slipping backwards instead.

The reason for this is that most collaboration or change management training tends to work from a place of buy-in rather than stay-in. Buy-in is slippery: stay-in is sticky. I'll explain.

If you've led a project or initiative, or a team, you'll know the importance of buy-in. It's that moment when people commit to the project and offer assurances that they will support it and do what they say they are going to do.

But when the agenda changes for the stakeholder, and previous commitments are no longer such high priority, they get off the bus. Sometimes they tell you they're out, sometimes they even ghost you – but ultimately you've lost buy-in, and it's through no fault of your own.

That's why we don't want buy-in. We don't want them sitting passively on the bus.

We want stay-in. We want them to want to drive the bus, or maybe even own the bus. We certainly don't want them to hop off any time the road gets bumpy.

How do we create a sense that all the parties have made a good deal and are better off with this arrangement than they would be without it?

The secret to moving past buy-in and into stay-in, is to unlock a level of motivation in your co-collaborators that is self-sustaining – that is, that they want success as much, if not more than you do. This will harness their goodwill, energy and commitment far more than you could do with any other method, and it reduces your personal effort in driving for results. You

> The secret to moving past buy-in and into stay-in, is to unlock a level of motivation in your co-collaborators that is self-sustaining – that is, that they want success as much, if not more than you do.

> 'Leaders who are frustrated by a lack of collaboration can start by asking themselves a simple question: What have they done to encourage it today?' – Francisco Gino

have real partners, and you are all driving just as hard for a shared outcome.

There are three gears (and two I recommend) to use when driving this bus. Win/lose, win/win and win neutral.

Win/Win

Our natural tendency is to distrust or disregard others' agendas. We also think more about our needs – what we'd like to say or what we need to achieve – than the needs of others. So how might we practise a more win/win approach to managing outcomes?

Resist the urge to talk

Leaders are taught to obsess about how we present; in meetings, public forums, and on social media. That means we think a lot about how to make the right impression. As a result, when others are talking we are more often planning what we are going to say than truly listening.

So our first job is to resist the urge to talk. I know this sounds out of context when the chapter you're reading is 'Make the case'. Surely staying silent doesn't make a case – so is that a conflicting message?

It would be if the art of making the case was the art of making *your* case, instead of making *the* case. To get stay-in rather than just buy-in, you have to master the latter (which requires listening) rather than the former (which requires talking).

Value questions over answers

When we are in charge of how the work gets done, we build a reputation as an expert. Experts know the answers, so they don't ask as many questions. They also tend to assume they are right and switch into solution mode far too quickly. Have you ever felt the rest of the room isn't keeping up? That the answer is so blindingly obvious to you that it's hard to contain your frustration? It's likely that you are still focusing on outlining your solution rather than understanding the problem.

To let go of this conditioning, focus on the implications of words, not just your assumptions about their meaning. It may mean you ask what you (as an expert) might consider stupid questions at times. For example, 'What does that mean in this context?' when you are pretty sure you know the answer. You may get an unexpected answer highlighting a misalignment that could later have been a significant derailer. Or ask, 'Why is that important?' to uncover an impact you didn't know about. In his book, *Humble Inquiry*, Edgar Schein writes that to get someone to stay-in and build a truly productive relationship, you must understand their needs intimately, and you can only do so through questioning (Schein, 2013).

Listen by watching

We often observe behavioural clues but don't act on them. Think of the last time you observed a colleague being hesitant about saying something, or a reaction that suggested a disagreement.

(Eye-rolling anyone?) Getting these things on the table is essential to making sure you have true stay-in – otherwise, you might be agreeing at a surface level and ignoring the clues that there is disagreement beneath the surface.

But how do we do this in the right way?

Showing empathy and humility makes this easier for both of you. That might be something like 'This is complicated, isn't it?' Or, 'I noticed your voice was a bit tentative on that last topic as if you weren't entirely sure. Shall we spend a bit of time working it through?' or 'You looked like you wanted to add something just then, what are your thoughts?'

Find common ground. Outline your challenges and ask them to do the same, looking for common pain points and problem statements. A shared problem statement, prioritised equally means that you are already shaping a mutually beneficial outcome. If you are both equally motivated by making that outcome a reality, then you have a strong foundation. If one person feels their problem is less valuable or less valued, then find other opportunities to make up the shortfall. Equity and fairness are important in collaboration – everyone needs to feel they are truly winning, not just playing the game.

Add instead of detracting from the conversation. Avoid sentences that start with 'no' or 'yes but', as these close contribution down rather than enhance and promote it. To get stay-in you want people to feel they are acting on their idea rather than on yours. This is one way of getting them to drive the bus rather than be a passenger. Use 'yes and' to expand on their idea and show your alignment to it. This will make them feel safe and supported; even if you took their idea in a slightly different direction.

Get specific. Many leaders are not good at asking for what they need. They either don't speak up, (and we will cover this in Managing Up), or their ask is ambiguous.

Have you ever heard the line: 'We don't have the capacity to do that.' What do you hear? That they are not willing, or that they are willing, but don't have capacity? The answer can be either.

What most people hear is resistance – that the speaker is not willing. So most leaders seek to address that with persuasion, hoping to make them become more willing. In the case where the speaker is willing but has a capacity constraint, this approach can make them feel badgered and railroaded into doing it – you'll lose their good will, even if they do agree to do it.

A smarter question might be: 'Is capacity is the issue, or are there other considerations at play?' to try to identify what needs to be addressed – capacity or willingness.

The speaker could have been more specific from the outset by making their needs clearer: 'I am very keen to do this but we would need another headcount to make that possible.' This way the focus of the conversation centres around a solution to getting that headcount, which is a more collaborative approach than that of persuasion.

Win/Lose

The win/lose approach is one that many are naturally inclined towards when entering a collaboration or a negotiation. This wrong-foots the relationship right away.

> 'Every win is an injustice to someone.'
> – Aristotle Onassis

When most people seek to influence an outcome, what they really mean is they are trying to get what they want. Getting what we want is not a bad thing – it's part of our role as B-Suite leaders to successfully represent the interests and agendas of our teams. However, this often means that most of us engage in collaboration or negotiation with a desire to win, and we unconsciously take an approach that asserts superiority or authority.

In a one-off transactional setting, it's a common negotiation tactic, but at work (or in relationships) it's a disaster.

It's logical that if someone wins and someone else loses, the loser is likely to be:

Resentful. Playing hardball usually means reprisals later on – we all have long memories and an inherent sense of fairness.

Resistant. You may win the battle, but you have lost the war. Can you expect cooperation and discretionary effort from someone down the track when you've made them feel they lost?

Rebellious. They may have lost this particular battle, but they might come back to challenge the outcome later on. And those who observed your method in the first bout (your teams, peers and leaders), may well support your opponent next time. Are you sure they admire someone who will burn bridges to get a win?

So when faced with a negotiation or collaboration that is a likely win/lose outcome, what can we do to make it work?

1. Separate the person from the problem. Don't let it get personal. It's the work that is causing the friction, not the two of you, so if you can stay focused on maintaining friendly terms, even in the most robust negotiation, then your conversation (and future relationship) has a fighting chance.

2. Assume good intent. No-one gets out of bed with the sole goal of irritating and thwarting you. Surprisingly, their world revolves around them, not around you. They are trying to do their best just as you are trying to do yours. So respect that, and work with it rather than against it.

3. Avoid assumptions. Humans love to find a cause or reason for a specific behaviour, even if we sometimes make it up! If someone is pushing back on an idea, don't assume you know why and project your assumptions into the conversation. For example, 'Jenny is resisting service level agreements because her team will never meet them' will deeply offend Jenny because her actual problem was that you were resisting reciprocal service levels for your team and that didn't seem fair. Assumptions can easily offend, but questions rarely do.

4. Focus on problems, not solutions. Don't come into your negotiation with a predetermined idea of the outcome. That would mean you are already focused on getting a solution over the line. And by design, this solution can

only possibly be right for you because you have not yet engaged your collaborators. If it favours anyone else, that's purely by accident, as it was invented by you and is therefore primarily for your benefit.

So stay away from starting at the end by presenting your solution. Instead, focus on your problem, seek common ground, and ask for ideas once you've determined if others share the same vested interest.

You'll probably find you come up with a solution that's quite different and does an even better job than what you had in mind. It also means that everyone is invested in the solution, which increases their sustained commitment to it beyond go live.

5. Be prepared to compromise. It's the nature of relationships and collaboration. The willingness to compromise – having a viable fall-back position – can give the illusion of a win/win even if there isn't one. This allows your negotiation partner to save face and feel you are both giving something to the equation. It avoids that sense of an unfair negotiation – which may create resistance based on that principle rather than the subject at hand.

For example, what if you wanted to eliminate 70 per cent of waste and can only get to 50 per cent? That's still a massive improvement for you, but a notable compromise from your original position, which will also make others feel they too are gaining something from the negotiation.

Win neutral

'Conversation means being able to disagree
and still continue the discussion.'

– Dwight Macdonald

A CEO client once told me that half the battle of leadership is keeping a conversation in neutral. This meant neither pushing for a win/lose nor seeking a win/win but simply striving for the absence of friction, obstacles or closed doors. Being in neutral is the third important gear to use when you want to drive the bus.

> Half the battle of leadership is keeping a conversation in neutral.

Ambassadors have long called this 'keeping the channels open', and its main purpose is to avoid a 'no' at all costs.

Dan Kahneman's research shows that losses loom larger than gains in human decision-making. Therefore when faced with uncertainty, a no is always more likely than a yes.

Kahneman also confirms that we like to suppress ambiguity and doubt, which means that once we have made up our mind, we are resistant to the idea of un-making it (Kahneman, 2011). The very act of un-making our mind increases mental stress levels (or cognitive dissonance, a term coined by Leon Festinger), so we resist letting it happen.

That's why so many people refuse to change their position digging their heels in when faced with incontrovertible facts and logic. It's simply too stressful.

So if you approach influencing as an exercise that is more about avoiding a no than getting a yes, you'll keep your options in play. And that means focusing on keeping the channels open rather than closing a deal.

Managing up

> *'The question isn't who's going to let
> me; it's who is going to stop me.'*
>
> – Ayn Rand

Most of us have an intense dislike for the term 'managing up', as it conjures images of greasy pole-climbers and upwardly mobile politico types. As we don't like to think of ourselves in this way, we shy away from taking action.

> Managing up
> doesn't mean
> sucking up.

This is a mistake. Managing up is important on every level, from improving your day-to-day performance or the important relationship with your boss, increasing your perceived value to the C-Suite, enhancing your earnings or securing seniority.

Managing up doesn't mean sucking up.

Managing up is just as important as managing outcomes, messaging or reputation. We can't leave our relationships with senior leaders to chance!

The good news is that you can stop thinking about becoming a snake oil salesman. It doesn't have to work that way.

Managing your boss

> *'The key to successful leadership*
> *today is influence, not authority'*
> – Ken Blanchard

If you didn't already know, the relationship with your boss significantly impacts your satisfaction, your effectiveness on the job and your career prospects (Pfeffer, 2010).

A study released by Keas.com found that 77 per cent of employees experienced physical symptoms of stress from bad bosses (Keas. com, n.d.). As a coach, I've certainly had my share of B-Suite leaders report having a bad boss – it's not an uncommon problem.

Yet as with any relationship, at least 50 per cent of the problem must be ours to solve.

When discussing this question with someone reporting a bad boss scenario, we frequently uncover a gap in one or more of the following mindsets:

- 'I need this: my relationship with my boss is key to my success.'

  What I often hear instead is: 'My boss should be better at managing me'. My advice is to shift the attitude – to recognise it as low accountability, a victim mindset and an inferiority complex. Your boss is absolutely central to your success, but unless that attitude changes, you will quickly become less than central to theirs. And that's not a good place to put yourself!

- 'This relationship is two way.'

While your leader has clearly articulated responsibilities to you (just as your position description makes clear your responsibilities to lead and develop your team), your responsibilities to your leader are less well-defined. We rarely run training courses on how to be a great direct report, but there are plenty on how to become a great leader. The problem is that we have a social contract that is not two-way. Your expectations of them are clear, but you don't have the authority to enforce them. Their expectations of you are not clear, yet they do have the authority. That is likely to mean the balance is out unless you take the proactive stance that every good relationship is a two-way street.

- 'My boss has a lot on their mind, and much competition for their time.'

Another complaint I hear is 'I haven't had a catch-up with my boss for weeks' or 'My boss keeps cancelling our catch-ups'. In response to this, I ask why exactly you need the catch-up? The reactions range from blank looks to 'I just need to talk to them', to specific questions. Being a little more empathetic and smart about your time with your boss will mean you can handle getting less of their time,

> Being a little more empathetic and smart about your time with your boss will mean you can handle getting less of their time, yet they'll prioritise you more highly.

yet they'll prioritise you more highly. This section will show you how.

To balance your relationship with your leader and give both of you what you need, approach regular catch-ups with the following model in mind:

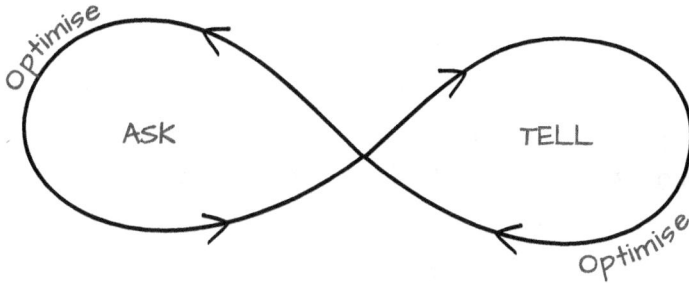

Figure 12: Managing your boss

Ask

'What do you need from me?' can be one of the most difficult questions that early stage leaders hear from their boss.

> My client Melissa called me in a fluster before one of her skip meetings saying: 'I know my Director's question will be 'What do you need from me?' What a ridiculous question. If I knew what was needed, then I would have fixed it myself.'

This is a common reaction, that comes from a complicated place. You want to look good, so you'd rather not ask for anything. After all you want them to know that you're taking action on your own. And this autonomy is fine *inside* your own team, but your manager already knows you have that under control. What they are really asking is what's going on *outside* your team that might be getting in your way, and what can they do to help. Think of everything that is outside your sphere of control – but might be in theirs. This could be clients, collaborators or other teams in a supply chain that are making it difficult for your area to perform effectively or have as much impact as you would prefer.

This is a great way to use one-to-one time most effectively. High impact leaders don't need a lot of individual time with their leader, and often release them from that commitment when they recognise and respect that their boss is busy too. Instead, they focus on being explicit about what they need to ask so that they receive optimal value from their boss in the limited time available. They also have less need to respect strict catch-up regimes because they pinpoint their asks. They know they can get a decision over a short call or email rather than wait for an in-person catch-up.

> Senior leaders spend an incredible amount of time managing perceptions and are grateful when you are attuned to this part of their role.

Tell

Another way to ensure your catch-ups are valuable from your manager's point of view is to determine what they need to be told. Typically this will fall into a few buckets that are heavily risk and reputation in flavour. I call them aircover, no surprises and what's next.

Senior leaders spend an incredible amount of time managing perceptions and are grateful when you are attuned to this part of their role. In a way, this is you helping them to manage up. Even at C-suite level, it doesn't stop.

Provide air cover

We frequently do this so we can buy ourselves (and our teams) space to let reality catch up with perception. In his book, *The Prepared Investor*, Christopher Manske calls this perception trumping reality, and says it affects stock markets in the same way as stakeholders. People react to what they think is occurring, which isn't necessarily the same thing as what's actually happening (Manske, 2020).

A classic example of this is where something has gone wrong, and your team needs room to fix it. But bombarded by client and stakeholder enquiries means they don't have time. Hence the problem appears (and proceeds to become) larger and more impactful than it really is. Of course, the potential reputation damage is also significantly worse than it needs to be. Your leader's role in this situation is to provide you air cover — a protective barrier so that you can get the job of fixing done, instead of the job of managing enquiries.

No surprises

Few people like surprises — even surprise birthday parties or engagements are likely to get an emotional response as our brains react to surprise with fight or flight. So it's no secret that one of the things most senior leaders find hard to forgive is a nasty surprise. They absolutely loathe finding out from someone else that there is a problem in their patch. It makes them feel incompetent (yes, they too have inner confidence issues), and it naturally makes them question your competence.

There are typically three scenarios that create such surprises:

- You knew but failed to tell them. That makes them question your accountability or bravery.

- You knew but thought you could get it back under control before anyone noticed. That makes them question your judgement.

- You didn't know. That makes them question your controls and operational oversight.

In my experience, what is least forgivable is not a lack of accountability, judgement or operational excellence – it's lack of communication.

A leader with poor communication skills is a frustration to their teams and a liability to their leader.

Instead, raise the risk, state what you are doing about it and outline anything you need from your boss.

Optimise

Flowing constantly between ask and tell, work is still needed to build a trusting relationship with your leader, and that's a two-way street. Make sure you're thinking about how you can work together better – how you can optimise your relationship.

> Treating your relationship with your boss as a project of its own will reap rapid rewards.

Treating your relationship with your boss as a project of its own will reap rapid rewards:

- For you in the long run. They are more likely to advocate for you and let you deputise for them when the time comes.

- For your team. You'll get far greater insight with this model, which will help your team to feel secure in your direction-setting.

- And for your day-to-day performance. You'll spend less time second-guessing their needs and have more confidence that you have their trust.

Get your approach right

Check in with your leader on their preferred M.O.

- How you structure your agendas
- How you build your reports and insights
- What is their preferred approach to receiving a brief and who should have read it before them?
- How do they like to communicate, and what time of day is best?
- How they consume information – are they a visual, or a numerical reader?

Knowing these preferences will help you to avoid the frustration of 'they just don't like my approach' and optimise your efforts.

How you brief your Executive when requesting their time is another great way to optimise your relationships. The former Executive General Manager of a well-known retail bank shared a formula that she was taught to use on her route to the C-Suite.

- Purpose. Be clear on the purpose of your meeting; is it to inform, sign off, consult or negotiate – and on what topic?
- Product. What outcome do you seek from this involvement?
- People. Who else needs to be involved and why?

- Process. Is your ask for a short or long meeting, a one-off or a repeat such as a board or committee?

- Preparation. Do you need your Exec to prepare anything for the meeting, and if so how much time should they allocate to it (for example, reading time) or what key messages do you want shared (if they are speaking)?

Get your tone right

Most leaders both respect and fear the hierarchy, and this can drive us to adopt or magnify certain styles when we deal with more senior leaders. Have you sometimes felt tongue-tied with one senior leader when you feel perfectly comfortable and chummy with another? Style plays an important role in our relationships. Here are the most frequent stylistic mistakes that I see in managing up.

Don't be fighty:

- Aggressive/dominant behaviours do not impress senior leaders. It marks you more often as a pain in the neck than as a firebrand. Instead, smile, relax and listen very carefully. Your path to influencing a senior person will rarely be to use force – they've seen that tactic before and will simply block your access to certain conversations to keep you in your box.

- Passionate/rigid perspectives are naive. Sticking to your guns is not always seen as a strength – especially when leadership involves so much negotiation and compromise. If you can't have an open mind, keep your emotions out of it, and be prepared to give a little ground, then you are not showing executive potential. Instead, balance having a point of view with holding onto that point of view lightly, be prepared to give in order to get.

- Overly friendly/familiar approaches can backfire. Your Exec is not your best friend, so calling them 'mate' or shortening their name without invitation is often seen as an affront. It's something I've often heard laughed at behind closed boardroom doors. And if your Exec is actually your best friend, then keep familiarity for the weekend. Showing it at work will either alienate your colleagues or suggest your Exec is cool with being treated like a chum by others.

- Make their life easier. No manager (including you) wants to drag someone along with them, arguing and pushing back all the way. It's like taking a dog for a walk when they really don't want to go. In the end, the walks stop, or you get another dog, so if you're dragging the chain, best stop.

When I remember the stand-out members of my leadership team, they always started every response with 'Yes'. Sometimes that was 'Yes and... here are the risks', or 'Yes and... have you thought about this?' But ultimately they always started with Yes, and that created a can-do relationship that really took the team – and our relationship – places. No chain-dragging there.

Cialdini's first principle of persuasion states that human beings are wired to return favours and pay back debts – to treat others as they've treated us. Being a big supporter of your boss makes it significantly more likely that they will be a big supporter of you in return (Cialdini, 2007).

Don't be flighty:

- Take a position or have a point of view. Your Exec is paying you to think, so have a point of view to start the conversation with. Be prepared to be comfortable when questioned about it, and open to being convinced otherwise. If you go in with no opinion, you're asking them to do all the hard work, and they won't thank you for that. Offer your thought process: 'I'd be happy to walk you through my decision process and the other alternatives I considered.'

- Don't start your point with a preface or provide the backstory context first. Get to the point. Your Execs are ridiculously busy and have a million thoughts in their heads. I have often heard an Exec interrupt a direct report after a few minutes to say 'I'm sorry, but I still have no idea what we are talking about'. Instead, lead with a snappy headline that will help you get to the point fast. Your ability to communicate concisely is essential for influencing and communicating at all levels, so obsess about that opening statement, whether in person or by email. Any marketer will tell you that's key to engagement and to easier decision-making, which ultimately is what we are after with our bosses.

- Don't tiptoe around their feelings. No hedging or deferring, 'I think we should consider stopping this program ... unless you don't think so...' This is a frustration trigger for many executives who are concerned that you're making recommendations based on what you think they want to hear rather than what's best for the business. Of course, they'll tell you if they don't think so – that's what they are paid to do. Your job is to give them confidence in your judgement, so don't undermine yourself. Replace 'unless you don't think so' with 'I'd love to get your perspective'.

Bad bosses

'We judge ourselves by our intentions and others by their behaviour.'
— Stephen M.R. Covey

According to a global study by The Potential Project, 77 per cent of leaders believe they're doing a great job; and yet 65 per cent of employees said they'd forgo a pay rise to see their leader fired. That's right — to see them fired (Hougaard, 2018).

You might have a bad boss. You might even be one. But what's certain is that we will all have to deal with one at some point in our lives. We will have an interaction with a leader who was underwhelming, unimpressive or downright unacceptable. We've probably met a leader who's a bully, one who is irrational, incompetent or untrustworthy, and we remember how that made us feel; trapped and backed against the wall.

Mary Abbajay tells us 'Research shows that it takes up to 22 months to emotionally and psychologically recover from the trauma of a psycho, crazy, bully, tyrannical, screaming, egomaniac boss' (Abbajay, 2018). You may well think about forfeiting your next pay rise to see them fired, but there are other methods.

Why does a good boss turn bad?

These are stressful times. When levels of uncertainty and ambiguity are at an all-time high, people are keener than ever for answers. Being a leader yourself, you will know that correlates with the pressure on you to have those answers. And that's ironic, as the pressure to have answers goes up precisely because the availability of answers goes down. And you wonder why leadership is hard.

Moments like these make us feel defensive, anxious or scared, and it often shows in our interactions. It means we are contributing as much, if not more, to a difficult or frustrating relationship.

The thing is you, your team and your boss are all feeling the same way. So you're likely to spark each other off, and to deflect blame – which typically travels upwards.

Why do we blame leaders more?

As leaders, we are expected to rise above petty things such as emotion. We are told to control ourselves and to hold ourselves to a higher account than those around us. Sure, we get paid more, so we certainly have to earn it at times.

Even as a leader, or maybe especially because we are a leader, we can find it really hard to forgive our boss when they fall off their pedestal.

So what can we do about it?

- Use compassion. Why have they had a bad boss moment? How are they feeling? How can you alleviate that rather than contribute to it? What's going on with their boss? (I bet it's worse!) What does he/she need to return to normal?

- Try to imagine the most forgiving reason they could be having a bad boss moment. Is it truly their fault, or could it be something out of their control?

- Think strategically. What's really at play here? What do they want to happen? Just upsetting you is pointless and unlikely to be their true motive. What threats are they perceiving, and how might you present to them as non-threatening? If they're obsessing over something that makes no sense to you, then the chances are they are obsessing over the implications or perception of the thing, rather than the thing itself. It's like having an issue with wearing shorts at the office. It rarely has anything to do with your fashion choices; it's more likely to be about what others might think.

- Clarify. When people are frustrated or overwhelmed, they articulate poorly what they need. Think of how often parents say: 'Use your words' to a toddler who is getting red in the face. And faced with a frustrated leader, many of us tend to shy away or shut down. Yet this is the time to lean in and confirm your understanding. Affirmation not only reduces miscommunication in times of ambiguity and stress but it makes your boss feel heard and increasingly confident that you've got this.

- Be objective. Step back from your own emotions for a moment. 'Go high,' as Michelle Obama would say. This is unlikely to be about you. It's more about them, so don't take it personally. By looking at the situation from a distance, you can observe their behaviour until it feels less threatening.

- Get proactive. You can't control their reaction to the situation, but you can control your own. Put some structure around your interactions, so you feel less on the back foot all the time. Ask structured questions and explain your plan before they get going. Pre-empt their most likely triggers and get smart about them. Managing up means precisely that, not being passive about situations that you could, with a little forethought, avoid.

- Show leadership. A leader is a leader. Hierarchy be damned. If you need to lead a fellow human out of a bad situation where they are not coping, then go ahead and do it. Don't wait for them.

- Be human. Shake off the view that they know what's going on or that they have the authority. This simply isn't true in business any more. As a leader yourself, I imagine you already knew that. It's time to stop assuming your boss is all-knowing. Don't hesitate to offer up your knowledge, guidance and suggestions. You know you'd appreciate it were the roles reversed.

- Hold the mirror up. Bosses are human too, and we all have off days. If you're thinking 'My boss was having a bad boss moment last week', I'm not surprised. But are you sure it's your boss that's having the moment and not you?

As we start to change our operating state, it's a good time to review and re-set our relationship with hierarchical leadership. Most of us have a dose of both respect and fear towards the hierarchy – and therefore to those in more senior roles.

Does that fear and respect always serve us? I'd say no, especially not when you have a problem leader to deal with.

Yet it is inevitably true that we learn more about leadership under a bad boss than we do under a good one. That's because our best approach to managing a bad boss moment is to show great leadership – and it's especially critical when the boss is failing to do so.

Focus on the business case

'...Assume that you have a very brief time to make an impression, and that you'll be allocated a tiny amount of memory space in the overloaded and preoccupied brains of your audience.'

– Steve Woodruff

Business Cases are a classic vehicle for influence and one that people often get wrong. Google how to write a business case, and you'll learn exactly how to write one. But the act of writing anything down is almost the last thing you should do!

Instead, focus on your influencing. Work out what the key needs are, understand who you need to influence and how you're going to do it.

Work out the key needs

In my experience, stakeholders only buy for three reasons.

- Pain. Friction points, loss-making initiatives and service failures are classic examples of pain points that are large, well known and universally accepted. If you have a solution to address the pain, in full or in part, then you will have a receptive audience. Humans are wired to avoid pain more than to seek opportunity, so this is always the first place that I would expect to see an executive show interest.

- Fear. Compliance, legal and reputation risks are all high-interest points for company executives, some of whom can be personally liable for problems in this patch. Fear-based pitching is usually based on the 'Can you afford not to' frame. In his book, *Crossing the Chasm*, Geoff Moore recommends that we find something that absolutely terrifies them and pitch a solution to that (Moore, 2014).

- Opportunity. A rarer buying signal than fear and pain, but sometimes an executive will invest to make the most of a competitor's misfortune, or another situation will arise that you think is worth making a play for.

By spending time understanding what pain, fear (or opportunity) matters most to your stakeholders, you'll identify an issue that really resonates, rather than trying to persuade them to buy into a solution that they may not need. Too often, I see leaders decide they want to do or buy something and then shop around for a problem that matches that solution. This is often found in the world of 'best practice', and it's to be avoided. Don't be a solution looking for a problem.

> Don't be a solution looking for a problem.

The reason you need to align with well-known and inarguable pains or fears is that your influencing pathway will rarely follow the chain of command. Unless you are in a very simplistic organisation, pitching your solution to just one executive is not going to be enough to get it across the line.

Decide who matters

You need to influence the people who influence people. It used to be said that if you are not in the room, you are not in the deal, but this is no longer the truth. Sometimes your 'deal' will be considered, evaluated and discussed when you are not in the room. The broader your role becomes, the more comfortable you need to be with this if you are going to achieve impact at scale.

Become adept at identifying and navigating that invisible wall of influencers. I'll always remember the story of Bill Clinton's Chief of Staff, who tried to get the President to sign off an important new hire without getting Hillary Clinton across it first. Needless to say, that lesson was hard learned. There are plenty of Hillarys out there to influence on your way up the line. Be aware of them and include them in your plans wherever you can.

Most senior leaders have a trusted advisor who you should aim to influence, and they will have a bench of experts they'll run things past too. There's a whole network of mentors, sounding boards and character judges that your 'target' decision-makers will refer to. You have to get through them before you can get to your end goal. This invisible wall of influencers is impossible to fully map – it could be someone's sister or tennis partner who tips the balance. And this is why managing your reputation is so important, as it's the only way you can have confidence that this invisible wall of influencers will let you through (but more on that later).

One of the funniest stories I ever heard was from an aspiring senior leader who got trapped in the elevator with their CEO for two hours. Making small talk in an elevator was a genuine nightmare scenario for this leader, and yet here they were having the dreaded 'So what do you do' conversation with no chance of getting off at the next floor. As you can imagine, their conversation ranged pretty widely. Eventually, my client confessed to his CEO that he had an aversion to this kind of elevator pitch, and never knew what to say to an executive when travelling the floors even for a few minutes. His CEO told him that two minutes is far harder than two hours, and that he completely understood the feeling having had it himself for many years. His remedy? Tell them what you've done this week, what you're going to do next week and what that should achieve. Have that ready at the beginning of each week (or month, or quarter), and you'll always be ready for the dreaded question, 'So, what have you got going on?' next time you step into the lift.

Managing the messaging

'Wise men talk because they have something to say; fools, because they have to say something.'

– Plato

The way we manage messaging affects not only our teams' clarity but also their resilience, initiative and engagement. You can illustrate your point and build culture through the words you choose.

Four of the ten most important leadership competencies are attributable to communication (Giles, 2016).

Most of us focus our messaging on formal presentations or the written word, but of course, our teams are watching us all the time and hanging off every word. So watching our written and unwritten language in both formal and informal environments is just as important.

Leaders who have a great handle on managing the messaging can lead from a distance, building big teams and broad networks of stakeholders who are all on the same page. Those leaders who haven't got there yet can often find themselves working far harder, correcting the messaging, getting people back on the same page and unravelling misunderstandings. Your ability to manage the message conveys not only the content, but also the confidence, culture and reputation of yourself and your teams.

Whether spoken, written, or through your body language, managing your messaging is important all the time.

Written language

> *'They'll hear your content, but*
> *they'll smell your intent.'*
> – Georgia Murch (Murch, 2018)

We've all read leadership comms that are full of detail, right?
Did we remember them? Maybe for a short time.
Did we even finish reading them? Probably not.
Could we repeat them? No chance

As B-Suite leaders, it's our job to communicate in a way that informs, inspires, clarifies and motivates. And most of us don't have the benefit of a communications manager to do it for us!

Your written communications benefit from being more memorable — there's a lot of traffic to stand out in.

Make it memorable

- If you can't explain it, they won't get it.
- If they don't get it, they won't buy in.
- If they don't buy in, it won't get done.

Never put more than five bullet points on a communication. Why? People only have five fingers to tick off. Any more than that and they'll forget one of your points. So, if you want them to remember and repeat those points to others, then ticking off five points on five fingers (or three — the brain loves a three) is a way to train your brain's neuroplasticity, to learn new things. The fingertip receptors are literally a superhighway to the brain (it's why Braille is so amazing) so we should use this technique to make sure people get the message, remember it and repeat when we need them to.

Use rhyme or rhythm. Both create patterns that help us to recall the message more easily and for longer. It might sound a bit weird, but mnemonics are proven ways to help people to make sense of, compartmentalise and retain information. If you're sending out information and want it to be easily recalled, then stop and check what you are trying to achieve with your comms.

Think about it – I bet you can recall at least one nursery rhyme from childhood?

'In fourteen hundred and ninety-two, Columbus sailed the ocean blue.' And that might be from more than 20 years ago.

Can you recall your most recent internal comms from this week?

Make it simple

A common mistake is when leaders communicate with technical accuracy, rather than memorable simplicity. It's a tough task as simplicity is by far the harder pathway, but that's the key difference between leadership comms and instructional comms. Good leadership comms is about the *why* and a bit of the *what* – not the *how*.

> Good leadership comms is about the *why* and a bit of the *what* – not the *how*.

So next time you find yourself starting an email with 'how to do something', take a moment to think about 'why this is happening' followed by 'what to expect next'. You can always add the 'how to' section at the bottom, or provide a link to the instructions. It should not be the core of your messaging – and if it needs to be, consider a training course instead!

Make it easy

Remember to keep it feeling easy.

If it sounds easy, people will think it is easy.

If they believe it is easy, they are more inclined to try it.

So make it sound easy.

And make it look easy.

Something as simple as spacing, multiple fonts and length can turn people off. I bet you've come across those websites that make your eyes hurt, so your brain can't engage? Or a document that is so messy your brain rebels and doesn't even let you try to make sense of it? Simple things like layout and font choice can evoke a fight reaction that makes you actively dislike what you see, and therefore disinclined to action it. Imagine failing to influence based on something as simple as your choice of font!

- Keep your font simple, use bold and bullets to draw the eye deliberately (but never more than five).
- Don't scroll more than twice. If it takes that much, then it is too long and needs to be broken down. Use links or attachments instead of main body text.

Make it relevant

Add your B-Suite spin to your executive's top-down comms to help your teams to relate it to their roles.

As with many people, I've spent much of 2020 obsessing over the global pandemic.

To discover what was going on in Wuhan, the pandemic's ground zero, people had been turning to Tinder (Wilson, 2020). It reminded me of 9/11 when people watched citizen reportage via YouTube and Facebook before watching the mainstream news.

Then I read Gartner's HR priorities for 2021, and was captured by their insight that top-down communications lower engagement and hasten change fatigue (Gartner, 2020).

Top-down comms are often not enough – side-on comms are needed too. That's because top-down has to be generic when most people want specifics – a citizen's report.

So our B-Suite spin is necessary to help translate top-down and generic comms into personalised and specific conversations. We can enhance engagement and stave off change fatigue with that one little tweak.

Body language

> *'The most important thing in communication*
> *is hearing what isn't said.'*
> – Peter Drucker

Body language is a simple yet often under-managed factor that can make or break leadership influence.

Dan Kahneman calls the brain 'a machine for jumping to conclusions', and notes that the machine gets one of its most powerful signals in the first seven seconds of an interaction. The non-verbal first impression (Kahneman, 2011).

The brain is wired to make snap decisions, judgements and to label you at a gut-instinct level.

> Body language is a simple yet often under-managed factor that can make or break leadership influence.

If we walk into a room carrying the wrong vibe, it's incredibly difficult to overcome. In fact, it's more than five times harder to overcome an initial first impression, and until then, you are viewed through a filter – a bias that you have introduced through your body language.

So think about your preferred filter. Do you want to be timid and apologetic, or confident and compassionate?

Attitude and mindset shine through body language, and only the most skilled can truly master it. Think about poker players who are famous for their lack of body language, yet even the greatest of those will have a 'tell'.

One of my mentors taught me to slow right down when I was feeling frantic. That the body language associated with feeling pressure – walking and talking too fast, thinking instead of listening and letting our hand signals magnify – were signals that would infect my team. And she was right, so now, the higher the pressure, the slower I walk, the deeper I talk and the more still I am with my signals. My team reads that I am not flustered, and remains calm, whereas before we all ran around like headless chickens.

Your body language can significantly affect those who have known you for ages. They know you even better than you know yourself so are likely to perceive even smaller clues about your state of mind. They'll guess where you're coming from before you even open your mouth.

Getting your mindset right isn't just for new impressions – it's for *all* impressions.

Watch your posture

Research by Dr Amy Cuddy, at Harvard University, confirmed that opening up your body to create space around you activates a sense of power so compelling it superseded known hierarchical levels. Simply put, confidently owning your space and spreading out a bit made people think you were more senior even when they knew you weren't (Elsesser, 2018).

> Women, take note: The average temperature in offices is set to 21 degrees. While it is the optimum temperature for men to work – it's a touch too cold for most women. This is a major reason why women tend to huddle and hunch up in the boardroom instead of stretching out like everyone else. Get ahead of this with the right clothes or assert your rights to a higher temperature.

Your body language can undermine your spoken words. If you're lacking conviction or delivering a message you are not aligned with, it will show. You'll drop eye contact or touch your neck, nose or eyes. At best, this signals you are not 100 per cent comfortable with what's being said. At worst, it signals you can't be trusted, and so we are back to that labelling thing again.

Using gestures makes you seen as warm, energetic and agreeable, and not using them suggests you are cold, analytical and logical (Kinsey Goman, 2010).

We should use gestures according to the impression we seek to make. Being naturally energetic, if I was going to a boardroom meeting, I'd deliberately slow my pace, still my gestures and calm my mind. When going on stage, however, I do the opposite, first doing star jumps to ensure I am expansive and energised so that people can feel the warmth and confidence from the back of the room.

> Clive is an accountant and notoriously still in his body language at work. People have labelled him as cold and unresponsive when he's the opposite when you get to know him – but the labels are in place before that can occur. So, Clive bought a pair of glasses (which he doesn't need) to have a prop that helped him move more. He used his glasses to point at things (rather than his finger), cleaned them as a way to have warm eye contact with someone and he would place them, folded on the table as a signal that he wanted to speak. Clive's popularity increased, and he found himself more warmly included in conversations.

Watch your hands

It's not just for gangster movies, hands below the table can trigger subconscious threat alerts as it looks like you're hiding a weapon! Keep them where people can see them. Another weapon is the pointed finger; so best to keep that holstered too partner.

But don't let those hands get too high or people will think you're gesticulating wildly. Keep them below shoulder height, somewhere above the desk-top and your shoulder.

> Sonia, a senior leader, was given feedback that she was scary, unapproachable and seemed to glower at people. She was quite shocked, so asked around – did other people see her this way? It turned out they did. Sonia's tendency to concentrate on the speaker in the room made her lean forward, drop her chin and pin them with her dark, intelligent eyes. It was quite terrifying if you

didn't know her, and off-putting even if you did. The irony was that Sonia intended this as a show of support, giving the speaker her full and undivided attention.

Sonia quickly learned to present in a more relaxed and offhand manner, so that the speaker relaxed too, and instead of silent concentration, she would ask questions, nod and smile. The results were rapid and remarkable. She was invited to join collaboration and governance boards and is sought after for her opinion.

As a rule, we have to watch our language 24/7, but the great news is that by doing so, we can hugely increase our cut-through, thus needing to correct others less frequently. You'll rarely be happier than when you see one of your leaders explaining to their team how to remember and tell their customers the five most important things – when it's exactly what your email was trying to get across. Imagine when your stakeholders are faced with your team repeating the phrases and even ticking off the five points you used at a recent presentation. Will they think you're running a cult? No! They'll be impressed with how well you align people around your messaging.

As a rule, we have to watch our language 24/7, but the great news is that by doing so, we can hugely increase our cut-through, thus needing to correct others less frequently.

Manage your reputation

*'It takes 20 years to build a reputation
and five minutes to ruin it.'*

– Warren Buffett

> Reputation is our number one asset as a B-Suite leader.

Reputation is our number one asset as a B-Suite leader. It dictates what people think of us, how they behave around us, and how highly they value us. It impacts the reputations of those around us – our team, our boss and our employer. Reputation has a proven impact on career prospects and on our ability to influence others.

You're senior enough to be watched all the time, which means you're already visible by the nature of your B-Suite role. Yet many of us go about our work with little thought about how we are seen, observed, and judged.

Most leaders dislike the concept of managing their reputation. They shy away from personal branding and shudder at the thought of self-promotion.

- We believe our work should speak for itself
- Because we hate self-promotion – it's icky
- We are terribly busy and just don't have time
- Perhaps, in your heart, you don't think you're clever or interesting enough

- Or maybe you're worried that no-one will listen if you start to speak out.

Let's take a look at the profiles of some of the greatest leaders in the world. Do you think that Steve Jobs, Angela Merkel, Richard Branson, Nancy Pelosi or Taylor Swift leave their reputation to chance? Of course not, and neither should you.

You may not aspire to be as famous or influential and that's okay – but here are some other reasons that might convince you to manage your reputation more proactively.

- Your team needs you to lift their profile because it makes their jobs easier if their reputation precedes them. As a B-Suite leader, part of *your* job is *their PR*. If you care for your team, you'll promote their reputation.
- Your boss wants to hear of your successes – it makes them look good!
- Your confidence will improve if you talk about your achievements more often, and if you don't value you, no-one will!
- Your career. Research shows that 90 per cent of executive recruiters review your reputation as part of their market research (Jacobs, 2013).
- Your stakeholders respect it. You are more likely to influence them if your positioning precedes you.

In a nutshell, building your reputation will help you to craft your confidence, realise rapid returns, and build belief in your business.

Follow the formula

'In an increasingly connected and transparent world, keeping a low profile is no longer an option for business leaders.'

– Weber Shandwick

The good news is that building a reputation isn't rocket science; it's about following a formula and applying it consistently. Once you've got that, then you should find that reputation building is neither hard nor terribly serious. Lighten up and have some fun with it, or you'll either come across as precious (not a great leadership brand), or you'll never build your reputation at all.

In his book, *Known,* Mark Schaefer describes committing to five rules of reputation-raising to succeed.

1. It's not about passion. Especially not as a B-Suite leader.
2. It is about being purposeful with your activity. Know *who* you are targeting, *why* you are targeting them and *what* they need that you have to offer.
3. There is no overnight success. This is about being consistently visible.
4. Be in the right space. Pick the right platform for you.
5. You don't have to be an expert to build a reputation. This is a key barrier for many people who feel that they are not smart enough, or interesting enough or 'stand out' enough. But you only have to be brave enough to comment on how you see the world through *your* eyes. No-one has your perspective (Schaefer, 2017).

Know your value

'Sometimes it helps to take the
self out of self-promotion.'
– Amanda Blesing

We have to become an authority on ourselves and be clear on our value and our value proposition.

You know how it is easy to talk at length about what you *know* or what you've *done*, but really hard to talk about *you*?

It's like being too close for comfort.

To help with that, I often consider my reputation as a product – or indeed an asset – rather than me. It helps to keep it at a distance and stops it all becoming too icky.

> We have to become an authority on ourselves and be clear on our value and our value proposition.

To do this, get clear on these key questions:

- Get a clear picture of your target audience. What do they need and how can you/your team meet that need?
- Remember your purpose. Who do you want to be noticed by and for what purpose?
- What is different about you/your team that means you will solve a problem better than others?
- And finally what would have happened had you not been there? What value and accomplishments would the company have gone without?

One of my clients, Sam, recently nailed his elevator pitch with 'My team has a reputation for creating value in a short timeframe. I know we're struggling with making a decision on X at the moment. Did you want us to have a look at it?'

A team I once worked with had a pretty clear value proposition. 'We're the best Devs there are, but we like to work our way. If that's okay, you'll get a great product. If it's not, get other Devs.' It sure was ballsy, but it worked.

At this point, I know you think this all feels too hard. But you'd persevere with a value proposition if it was for a business case, or a product wouldn't you? If you were crafting a deck for your Executive to let you do something, or pitching your Board? Making the case for your reputation, and actively managing it, is an essential part of your toolbox too. Neglecting reputation can be *far* more impactful than neglecting to nail a business case or pitch.

It doesn't have to be complicated – it just has to matter to the people who matter to you.

Be visible

'The power of visibility can never be underestimated.'

– Margaret Cho

Once you've got a simple handle on your value proposition, you amplify it.

Over lunch with a client, she let me into a secret. She loathes self-promotion and wishes her work would speak for itself. But she still prioritises reputation-raising.

'Despite my busy schedule, I drag myself to do one thing a week, just to stay visible,' she told me. She recently landed a huge promotion into a target industry, and her reputation definitely preceded her into that role. 'It's not about me; it's about developing my reputation as an asset, so my company and my team benefit.'

The highest-earning executives in your country are likely to be names that you know. If you're highly valuable, but no-one knows it, then there's a chance that you're not that valuable after all.

Social media

Social media straddles both internal and external audiences and is an easy way to establish a name for yourself and your team's great work. Get yourself interviewed on a podcast or quoted in an article. You won't have to put too much thought into this, and it reflects well on both you and your employer. A thoughtful response to an industry post or a short post of your own celebrating a project, milestone, metric, or person is another easy way to be visible as a leader in your field.

External visibility

Public speaking opportunities often scare at first, so it's worth starting small and working up to a place where you are comfortable. We don't all want or need to be keynote speakers, so consider joining a roundtable to converse in a closed audience. Sit on a panel (a roundtable with more people watching), or do a fireside chat (a round table of two) to build your confidence.

There are plenty of opportunities to grow confidence without getting on stage at your industry's peak body. The thought of presenting to a room full of other experts is probably the hardest place to begin, so don't feel you have to start there! Your vendors, other smaller professional networks and conference break-out rooms (instead of the main stage) are all easier places to start.

Some businesses are not very media-friendly, but there is still plenty you can do to become more visible in your field.

Networking events and meet-ups take a bit of time out of your day, but they are often worth it. Not only do you have a chance to learn something new from the speakers, but many great industry collaborations and talent exchanges could not have happened if two leaders hadn't got talking over a networking lunch.

Don't forget your internal stakeholders too. You will become more visible to them if you are somewhat active online, well networked in your industry, and speaking or being quoted in a few forums. Leverage and accelerate that visibility internally at the same time.

Internal visibility

Through your day-to-day role, you can ask to be included in broader committee and governance forums or to chair certain panels and working groups. Present a relevant update or report (even an industry report) to your Executive.

You can also create broader visibility by sitting on diversity, CSR or community panels and playing a part in company events (such as MC'ing) for townhalls or leadership roadshows.

It's likely that, if you haven't tried to do something like this before, you might not be comfortable with the idea of communicating your value to others – even co-workers. Try floating out a small win over coffee and see what the response it.

Amazon Founder and CEO, Jeff Bezos, is widely quoted as saying 'Your brand is what people say about you when you're not in the room.' If only a small roomful of people know you, then that's not going to go far enough.

Ask for help

You need other people to say it more than you do. We all know the leader who is a blatant self-promoter. This full-frontal version of reputation management gives senior leaders plenty of clues about this person's style as a leader – and it won't be something many of them admire as it shows a lack of tact and shrewdness that they typically value.

Having others do your promoting for you is far more powerful, more believable, more broadly spread and way less effort for you. The easiest way to encourage them to promote you is to promote them first – remember if you *give* credit you tend to *receive* credit.

Ask others to help with your efforts; most people are happy to do so if they are clear on what you want (and happier still if it's not just about you!). Internal comms teams are often grateful if you can help out with an event or can step in for an interview.

Bear in mind that your wins are also your boss's wins – make sure they hear about them.

Not so long ago, I was lucky enough to have a fantastic boss who really elevated the reputation and profile of those working for her.

This hadn't happened to me before, but rather than decide that all my previous managers had been evil megalomaniacs, I did some self-reflection.

It turns out I had made one simple mistake; I had never asked for their help.

You might think that a great manager shouldn't need to be asked, but it's not their job to promote you – it's yours.

They can help. A lot. And most are motivated to do so. Why? Because if you look good, they look good.

Basking in the reflected glory of their direct reports does not hurt the leader one jot. Anyone paying attention will assume part of your success is their remarkable leadership, and they don't have to say a word about themselves to win that reputation.

So go for the win/win.

Whether you're a start-up, an aspiring senior leader or Kim Kardashian, manage your reputation deliberately. Be purposeful, talk at the level of your audience, pick the right platform and then persevere.

You'll find, after months of consistent hard work, that you're an overnight success.

Afterword

If you're in the B-Suite, you're in the middle of a whole heap of hard work, uncertainty and strain so I hope you found this book helpful.

If you're in HR, then you're struggling to determine the best way to support your leadership cohorts, and I hope this has given you some good ideas about where to start and who to prioritise.

If you're not yet in the B-Suite, you've probably discovered a few home truths about what your boss needs from you and what pressure they are under, and yet I hope you're still encouraged.

And if you're in the C-Suite reading this, I hope you've found some answers to the gaps in your B-Suite bench, and that it's given you some ideas on how to develop your future executives further.

About the Author

After a childhood of living around the world in Africa, the Middle East and Europe, Rebecca (who's from London) and her husband Steve (who's from Liverpool) made Australia their home in 2000. Since then they've added two new Australians to the mix.

Rebecca earned her stripes leading large teams in complex organisations and built quite a reputation for doing business differently. Today, she is among Australia's leading Talent and Leadership coaches and facilitators – helping leaders and their teams work.

She is particularly passionate about helping mid-level leaders, the B-Suite, to step up in the face of complexity.

Rebecca has been called the fairy godmother of middle management – although she's not sure how she feels about that!

If you're interested in learning more about Rebecca's programs, visit these links.

Level Up program:
https://boldhr.com.au/level-up-your-leadership/

Executive coaching:
https://boldhr.com.au/11-mentoring/

To get in touch directly with Rebecca, email:
rebecca.houghton@boldhr.com.au

References

Ahlvik, C. L. C. R. C. G. J. J. M., 2018. *Overworked and Under-Resourced: A Mindful Intervention for Middle Manager Well-Being.* [Online]
Available at: https://journals.aom.org/doi/10.5465/AMBPP.2018.14938abstract
[Accessed August 2020].

Baker, M., 2019. *Gartner Newsroom Press Releases.* [Online]
Available at: https://www.gartner.com/en/newsroom/press-releases/2019-07-22-gartner-survey-shows-only-half-of-business-leaders-fe
[Accessed August 2020].

Bersin, J., 2017. *Catch the wave: The 21st-century career.* [Online]
Available at: https://www2.deloitte.com/us/en/insights/deloitte-review/issue-21/changing-nature-of-careers-in-21st-century.html
[Accessed October 2020].

Davies, R., Lavandier, H. & Schwartz, K., 2017. *In search of a better stretch target.* [Online]
Available at: https://www.mckinsey.com/business-functions/strategy-and-corporate-finance/our-insights/in-search-of-a-better-stretch-target
[Accessed November 2020].

DDI, I., 2018. *Global Leadership Forecast 2018 Australia & New Zealand.* [Online]
Available at: https://media.ddiworld.com/research/global-

leadership-forecast-2018_au-nz-report_ddi_tr.pdf
[Accessed August 2020].

Deligkaris, P. P. E. M. A. M. E., 2014. *Job burnout and cognitive functioning: A systemic review.* [Online]
Available at: https://www.researchgate.net/
publication/262008721_Job_burnout_and_cognitive_
functioning_A_systematic_review
[Accessed August 2020].

Deloitte, 2019. *Leading the social enterprise: Reinvent with a human focus.* [Online]
Available at: https://www2.deloitte.com/ro/en/pages/human-capital/articles/2019-deloitte-global-human-capital-trends.html
[Accessed October 2020].

Folkman, J., 2015. *8 Ways To Get Work Done Faster.* [Online]
Available at: https://www.forbes.com/sites/
joefolkman/2015/03/23/8-ways-to-get-work-done-faster/#18352929495d
[Accessed August 2020].

Gladwell, M., 2005. *Blink : The power of thinking without thinking.* New York: Little, Brown and Co.

Goldsmith, M., n.d.. *Marshall Goldsmith quotes.* [Online]
Available at: https://www.brainyquote.com/quotes/marshall_
goldsmith_899359
[Accessed 2020].

Grant, A., 2016. *The Surprising Habits of Original Thinkers.* [Online]
Available at: https://www.ted.com/talks/adam_grant_the_

surprising_habits_of_original_thinkers?language=en
[Accessed August 2020].

Hanley, A. W. A. D. V. e. a., 2014. *Washing Dishes to Wash the Dishes: Brief Instruction in an Informal Mindfulness Practice.* [Online]
Available at: https://doi.org/10.1007/s12671-014-0360-9
[Accessed August 2020].

Hanson, R., n.d.. *Take in the Good.* [Online]
Available at: https://www.rickhanson.net/take-in-the-good/
[Accessed 2020].

Ibrahim, T., 2017. *The Secrets to Your Win: ...simple little things that make all the difference.* Newark, DE: Willow Books.

Kahneman, D., 2011. *Thinking Fast and Slow.* New York: Farrar, Straus and Giroux.

Kanter, R. M., 2009. *Change Is Hardest in the Middle.* [Online]
Available at: https://hbr.org/2009/08/change-is-hardest-in-the-middl
[Accessed August 2020].

Maslach, C. J. S., 1981. *The Measurement of Experienced Burnout.* [Online]
Available at: https://www.researchgate.net/publication/227634716_The_Measurement_of_Experienced_Burnout
[Accessed August 2020].

Mollick, E. R., 2012. People and Process, Suits and Innovators: The Role of Individuals in Firm Performance. *Strategic Management Journal, ,* 1 March, 9(33), pp. 1001-1015,.

Osterman, P., 2009. *Recognizing the Value of Middle Management.* [Online]
Available at: https://iveybusinessjournal.com/publication/recognizing-the-value-of-middle-management/
[Accessed August 2020].

Partnoy, F., 2012. *Wait: The art and science of delay.* New York: Public Affairs.

Sinek, S., 2009. *Start With Why: How great leaders inspire everyone to take action.* New York: Portfolio.

Stavroula, L. G. A. C. T., 2003. *OEH Stress.* [Online]
Available at: https://www.who.int/occupational_health/publications/en/oehstress.pdf
[Accessed October 2020].

Thornton, B., 2018. *blog.inspiresoftware.* [Online]
Available at: https://blog.inspiresoftware.com/7-statistics-leadership-development
[Accessed August 2020].

www.ingramcontent.com/pod-product-compliance
Lightning Source LLC
Chambersburg PA
CBHW050102210326
41519CB00015BA/3792